THE TRUTH ABOUT NATURE

A Family's Guide to 144 Common Myths about the Great Outdoors

Stacy Tornio and Ken Keffer

Illustrations by Rachel Riordan

FALCON GUIDES

GUILFORD, CONNECTICUT
HELENA, MONTANA
AN IMPRINT OF ROWMAN & LITTLEFIELD

FALCONGUIDES®

An imprint of Rowman & Littlefield
Falcon, FalconGuides, and Outfit Your Mind are registered trademarks of Rowman & Littlefield.

Distributed by NATIONAL BOOK NETWORK

British Library Cataloguing-in-Publication Information available

Library of Congress Cataloging-in-Publication Data available

ISBN 978-0-7627-9628-1 (paperback)

∞™ The paper used in this publication meets the minimum requirements of American National Standard for Information Sciences—Permanence of Paper for Printed Library Materials, ANSI/NISO Z39.48-1992.

The authors and Globe Pequot Press assume no liability for accidents happening to, or injuries sustained by, readers who engage in the activities described in this book.

MIX
Paper from
responsible sources
FSC® C005010

To Scott—one of those amazing, innovative, and clever teachers who goes above and beyond to get kids excited about nature and learning

CONTENTS

Spring

Summer

Autumn

Winter

ACKNOWLEDGMENTS

Thank you, Steve Tornio, for your endless support, ideas, grammar tips, and encouragement throughout all of our writing. You kept us on task more times than we'd like to admit, and you helped us brainstorm every subject matter possible (props for mosquitoes and the no-neck pig).

We also want to thank our agent, Uwe Stender. We lose track of how many times throughout the year we utter phrases like "Uwe is awesome" or "We're so lucky Uwe is our agent." We couldn't imagine a better literary partner. Thanks for helping us find our stride and encouraging us every step of the way.

This book is ten times better because of Katie Benoit Cardoso—truly one of the best editors that we have ever worked with. Katie, you challenge us, support us, and encourage us, and we are so grateful to work with you again. Thank you so much for seeing the need to get more kids and families outside. We're having a blast and are glad to share it with you!

Finally, we want this book to honor all those great teachers (both formal and informal) that have had a role in our lives. The role of a teacher is so important—kids listen to you . . . respect you . . . trust you. Believe us, they really do. If we can get teachers to help us dispel some of the myths in this book, then we know it will go to support our greater goal of getting kids outside and exploring the world around them without hesitation or fear. So in no particular order, here are some of the great teachers we've known over the years that we'd like to acknowledge: Linda Lancaster, Perry Bingham, Marjorie Bingham, Iva Bingham, Mrs. Pawlosky, Mrs. Price, Mrs. Tipton, Mrs. Sturdevant, Mrs. Murray, Mrs. Lanier, Miss Mueller, Mrs. Parker, Mr. Winland, Mrs. Neyer, Mr. Lussow, Hank Harlow, Merav Ben-David, Mark McKinstry, Brian Miller, and Kimberly and Kenn Kaufman.

FOREWORD

I have always been a teacher. When I was a little girl, around 6 years old, my sisters and I shared a bedroom with a huge chalkboard on one wall. I remember being surprised at how my two little sisters, Nancy and Susan, knew so little about the world around us. So I would take them to the best place for learning—outside. I loved those days. We dug with spoons in the dirt, caught frogs in the creek, made dandelion tiaras, played in the mud, ran through corn rows in our garden, and ate crackers under the fort blankets we strung in the bushes. This was all because I felt a need to teach them a thing or two. After all, it was my job to get them ready for school.

After I became a teacher for real, I discovered that I still had a job to do, and it wasn't that much different from when I was 6. I had to get kids outside more, and I had to teach them about this great natural world around us. This might seem obvious to some, but for the most part, kids nowadays are not kicked outside like we were. They aren't told to go out and explore on their own—to learn from the world around them. To me, this is a real shame, because I think all kids do some of their best learning when they're outside. I've seen this first-hand with hundreds of kids over the past twenty-five-plus years of my teaching career. When young people have a first-hand experience with nature, it creates lifelong learners, problem solvers, engineers, poets, scientists, mathematicians, writers, and thinkers. In short, nature is where we develop our roots.

This book, *The Truth About Nature*, provides an excellent springboard for developing those roots and getting you, your family, your students, or the young people in your life outside. As a teacher, I understand how important it is to have a good source to trust, and I can't think of a better book to recommend. Ken Keffer and Stacy Tornio are busting myths about nature. This is so important! We want kids to be outside exploring the world, not being afraid of it. Not only are they educating kids about essential subjects, they're doing so in a truly fun and exciting way. It's like an educator's dream! I hope you enjoy reading this book and testing out some of the myths as much as I did. I guarantee you will learn something. And I'm a teacher—I should know.

Hazel L. Scharosch
Project Learning Tree Outstanding Educator and Wyoming Game and Fish Conservation Educator of the Year

INTRODUCTION

It all started with a baby bird. Actually, to be more specific, it started with a question that pops up every single year about baby birds.

"If you touch a baby bird, will the parent abandon it?"

We were talking about this question around a campfire one night—about how it's one of the most common nature myths out there, yet it simply isn't true. (Seriously! A bird will not abandon its baby if you touch it. Read more about this one in the "Spring" section.)

As we talked more, we realized that the baby bird example is just one of many myths out there about nature. We started making a list, and pretty soon we had dozens of different examples and questions we could answer.

If you touch a toad, will you get warts?

If you cut a worm in half, will you grow two worms?

Will eating carrots improve your eyesight?

Is poison ivy contagious?

Can animals only see in black and white?

The answers to some of these questions might surprise you, which is exactly why we wanted to write this book! Many "facts" that kids (and adults) learn aren't true at all! A lot of times they get passed along from one person to the next because there's a tiny grain of truth to them. But in a lot of cases, there's a lot more myth to these things than fact.

It can be tricky to figure out what to believe. After all, the Internet has tons of information on nearly every topic imaginable. But that doesn't mean it's all true! This is where we can help.

From quirky fishing and gardening advice to myths that create animal misconceptions and fears, we think it's time to share the truth about the outdoors. With this book, you can uncover common myths about animals, plants, the ocean, space, the weather, and a whole lot more.

We want this book to get you thinking about nature in ways you've never imagined before. We hope it will serve as a resource for your entire family for years to come. We hope it'll set the record straight for many nature myths once and for all. And finally, we hope it gives you an excuse to get outside and explore on your own more than ever before.

We've always considered ourselves "play advocates," and we hope you use this book as an excuse to go play in the great outdoors. There's no better way to learn about the world around you than to experience it for yourself. So grab your book and head outside. We have a lot of myths that need to be busted!

TIPS FOR USING THIS BOOK

The core of The Truth About Nature is 144 myths, broken into seasons. Of course, not every myth fits perfectly into a season. Many cross over from one season to the next, but we think it offers a good way to really notice the world around you year-round.

It's important to remember that these myths aren't totally true. However, some of these myths have a little bit of truth to them, and we want you to learn this too. So we put together a myth scale, which will help you along the way. Take a look. . . .

Myth Scale

LEVEL 3. These myths are completely false. They are wrong on all levels, and there really isn't any truth to them.

LEVEL 2. These myths are mostly false. They might have a little bit of truth to them. It's easy to see how people might be confused by these myths, but don't be fooled. They aren't correct!

LEVEL 1. These myths aren't really true, but there's a lot more truth to them than the other myths. These are usually examples of how there are always "exceptions to the rule."

Even though this is a myth book, we have a lot more to offer! Take a look at these four additional features to look for.

Stranger than Fiction

Included in our "Stranger than Fiction" features are forty amazing facts about nature. Sometimes there are things in nature that sound so incredible that they *must* be made up. However, that's not always the case. You can find some pretty amazing facts out there about nature, and those are worth taking notice of too. Just remember these are facts though. Don't get confused about what's a fact and what's a myth!

Luck Legends

Look for sixteen "Luck Legends" that identify people and cultures that have superstitions on what to do for good luck—or at least to keep the bad luck away. We are not endorsing these as being true, but it's still fun to see the different types of beliefs out there when it comes to luck.

Weather Legends

We have sixteen "Weather Legends" too. It seems like everyone has a theory on how to predict the weather. Of course, we're not recommending you follow these either, but it's pretty entertaining to see all the different ways people use to try to figure out the weather.

Be a Scientist

Look for sixteen different activities and experiments labeled "Be a Scientist" throughout the book. Now you can bust a few myths on your own by testing them with a little science. Scientists have been doing this for years, and they'll often test and retest multiple times before coming up with a conclusion. Maybe it'll inspire you to come up with your own questions and experiments too!

Nature is pretty incredible, but don't just read about it. Get out there and experience it for yourself. If you do, you'll probably start to witness some "stranger than fiction" facts. Then you will start to recognize myths on your own too. But most importantly, you'll be connecting with the outdoors, which always leads to adventures and fun.

SPRING

1: Birds sing because they are happy.
MYTH SCALE: 2

About the myth: Have you ever been awakened early in the morning by the cheery songs of birds? You're all tired and groggy and perhaps not too happy to be awake so early. And what about the birds? They don't seem to notice you at all. They're just tweeting along like they don't have a care in the world. What are they so happy about anyway?

The truth: Birds wake up as soon as they catch a glimpse of sunshine. It might look like it's still dark outside to you, but they're ready to go as soon as the day begins. It's easy to think the birds are happy because they sound so jolly as they sing, but the truth is that birds don't have emotions like humans do. They're just singing because it's what they do.

The takeaway: Male birds are usually the ones that sing, especially in spring. They will sing early in the morning and throughout the day to try to catch the attention of a female or to stake their claim on a territory. Instead of being annoyed by the singing, see if you can figure out one bird song from the next.

Additional facts: A bird song and a bird call are two different things. A bird song is usually a series of notes (probably what you hear in the morning) by a male bird that is trying to attract a female. But a bird call is usually shorter and can mean a lot of things. Both males and females use calls to communicate. For instance, if there's a hawk in the area, birds will send out warning calls to other birds to stay away.

2: If you touch a baby bird, the parents will abandon it.
MYTH SCALE: 3

About the myth: You come across a baby bird that hasn't learned to fly yet. It's hopping about and seems scared. You look around and see a nest nearby, just at the crook of a tree. You want to help the baby, but then you remember some advice you heard about touching birds. It makes sense. You don't want the mother to abandon her baby because of you.

The truth: Bird parents have a strong instinct to care for their young, and they are not going to suddenly abandon it. For starters, a quick human touch doesn't actually transfer a very strong scent, so the parent bird probably won't even know you helped the baby back into its nest. Second of all, there are several examples of birds helping to care for young that aren't their own. For instance, brown-headed cowbirds will lay their eggs in another bird's nest, and then those birds feed and raise the young. Similarly, in bluebirds and others that nest more than once a season, juvenile birds will sometimes pitch in and help raise their siblings. So the bottom line is that a mother bird won't abandon her baby just because a human touched it.

The takeaway: If you find a baby bird on the ground, it's not necessarily hurt, lost, or abandoned. If you happen to see a nest nearby from which it likely fell out, go ahead and put it back inside. Of course, you shouldn't linger too long, because predators could pick up your scent and the parent is probably waiting to return. Otherwise, leave it alone and keep an eye out. Chances are its mom or dad will be back for it.

Additional facts: Most young birds don't actually spend that much time with their parents. You might think about young geese (goslings), and it certainly seems like they follow their mom around for weeks or even months. But this isn't the case for most young. Songbirds, which include most backyard birds, hatch and then leave their nest after only two to three weeks. Some of the bigger birds (owls, hawks, eagles) need to rely on their parents longer. Shorebirds often hit the ground running, leaving the nest as soon as they hatch.

Luck Legends

The sound of crickets chirping can be a soothing sound, and in some cultures, these insects are also good luck charms. So along those same lines, killing one would be very bad luck, even if the death is accidental. You'd better be extra nice to those crickets in your backyard!

3: Animals can smell fear.

MYTH SCALE: 3

About the myth: If you've ever been around a dog and are a little nervous (maybe because it's big or it doesn't look friendly), you know that it's nerve-racking. You try to make yourself calm down and act like the dog doesn't bother you, but that doesn't seem to work. It's like the dog can smell your fear.

The truth: It is true that all animals, including humans, have chemicals that come out of their bodies called pheromones. But the thing is, research shows that pheromones are something that only animals of the same species detect. This doesn't mean that the dog you're scared of doesn't know you're scared though. Chances are you are giving off other signs of being nervous, and it's picking up on physical clues instead.

The takeaway: The bottom line is that animals can't smell fear. Yes, they can detect when you are afraid, but that's probably because they can see it in your eyes, hear it in your voice, and detect it in your body language. Just try to act as confident as possible, and you'll be just fine!

Additional facts: Horses are another animal people say can smell your fear. This is not true either, but it's easy to see how someone might think so. When you're trying to ride a big horse, it can feel if you're nervous when you're sitting on top of it. It's how you hold the reins, kick your feet, and everything in between.

4: Female animals raise the young.

MYTH SCALE: 1

About the myth: Moms are pretty amazing, there's no doubt about it. Female animals will work for hours upon hours to prepare for their babies and then raise them, often without the help of a male at all. But just because this is common for many animals doesn't mean it's the rule. Males can be helpful too. It just depends on the species.

The truth: Let's look at birds for instance. Yes, many female birds, like hummingbirds, will build their nests and raise their young completely on their own. But then there are several species for which the males help out. Cardinals and bluebirds are a couple of examples of males that help throughout the process. In the mammal world, wolf fathers are an example of animals that help raise the young. They are very protective of their families and help teach the youngsters how to survive as they grow up.

The takeaway: If you see a baby animal with a parent, don't assume it's with the mom. Do a quick online search or find a good field guide to learn how different species raise their young.

Additional facts: Some male birds will help build a nest or feed the young, but it's the female that sits on the eggs, right? Not necessarily. Lots of male birds will take a turn sitting on the eggs, including great blue herons and mourning doves.

Stranger than Fiction

IF YOU SCARE AN OPOSSUM, IT WILL PLAY DEAD.

Opossums are pretty unusual animals. They are the size of small dogs and are pretty common in urban and rural settings. Like most animals, opossums can be pretty defensive when someone or something harasses or corners them. They'll bare their teeth and growl just like a dog, and they might also hiss. But their defenses don't stop there!

In many cases opossums will curl up and play dead. They do this because they hope predators will think they're dead and then will leave them alone. Have you ever heard the term "play possum"? It turns out it's a real thing!

In colder regions of the country, opossums often suffer from frostbite because they don't have a lot of extra fur to keep them warm. Don't be surprised if you see one with gnarly ears or a missing part of a tail in your area.

Luck Legends

SEEING A FROG MEANS WEALTH IS AROUND THE CORNER.

This is a great one! In addition to being symbols of wealth and prosperity, frogs have also been held in high regard as symbols of friendship. But let's get back to the wealth part. If this is true, then we'll all be going out on a frog hunt in spring!

5: Baby animals are helpless.

MYTH SCALE: 2

About the myth: Imagine you're outside going for a hike and you see a little bit of movement in the grass. You peer a little closer and see a baby deer (called a fawn) tucked down low. You worry a little bit, wondering if the parents have abandoned the baby. How is it supposed to survive all on its own? Shouldn't you help it?

The truth: It's easy to look at a baby animal and think it's helpless and abandoned, but this is not usually the case. For instance, a mother deer will find her baby a place to sit and hide from predators, but she's usually not very far away. You might find other animals like baby rabbits or birds this way too. Don't think they have been abandoned though. Keep an eye out, and you'll probably see the parents pretty soon.

The takeaway: Even if you don't see parents nearby, babies aren't necessarily helpless. There's often an awkward stage where young animals aren't babies anymore, but they're not adults yet either. They still have ways of protecting themselves though. It's best to just leave them alone and let nature take its course.

Additional facts: Some baby animals don't stay with their parents very long at all. Birds are on their own at a young age, and so are rabbits. Rabbits are only with their parents for about six to eight weeks, and then they're all alone!

6: All reptiles lay eggs.

MYTH SCALE: 1

About the myth: Lots of animals lay eggs, including birds, insects, fish, and reptiles. But do all reptiles lay eggs? Nothing is ever as easy as it seems. Of course there are a few reptiles in there that have to be different. Let's find out which ones they are.

The truth: Snakes are definitely reptiles, but not all of them lay eggs. Well, not in the traditional sense anyway. Many female snakes, including rattlesnakes and garter snakes, keep the eggs inside their bodies. So they're not really "laying" the eggs. Instead, the eggs hatch inside of the mother, and she keeps them in there until it's time for them to come out. Then when she gives birth, they come out of her alive! Can you imagine a female snake slithering around with eight to ten babies inside of her? It sure makes it hard to move around and catch food.

The takeaway: Don't assume that all reptiles are egg layers! You can impress your friends or even your teacher with cool facts like this.

Additional facts: Snakes aren't the only exception to reptiles laying eggs. Skinks are another reptile that sometimes delivers live babies. Skinks are a type of lizard. Yes, some lay eggs in the traditional way, but not all do!

Luck Legends

IF YOU SEE A RAINBOW, YOU WILL HAVE GOOD LUCK.

Rainbows can brighten anybody's day. They aren't all that common, so it's really special when you see one. Some people even like to make a wish when they see a rainbow. Whether you believe this one or not, maybe just seeing a rainbow will inspire you to make your day lucky!

Stranger than Fiction

TEMPERATURE DETERMINES WHETHER ALLIGATOR BABIES ARE MALE OR FEMALE.

When it comes to alligators having babies, they're a lot like birds. They build nests and lay eggs. Female gators build up large mounds of mud and natural vegetation, and they do all of this work mostly at night. After the female lays her eggs, she will add even more mud and vegetation on top. Then the eggs stay in there for about sixty-five days.

During this time (called the incubation period), something really cool happens. If they incubate at temperatures below about 86 degrees Fahrenheit, the baby gators will be females! And if the temperature is above about 91 degrees, they will be males! It's pretty amazing to think you're going to be a boy or a girl just based on how hot or cold it is!

Alligators can lay as many as ninety eggs at once, and they have a tougher, more leathery shell than the eggs you might have in your refrigerator.

7: You can only see a rainbow after it rains.

MYTH SCALE: 1

About the myth: This myth is a little tricky because rainbows do often come out after it rains. Here's the thing though—these aren't the only times you can see a rainbow.

The truth: Yes, rainbows come out after a rain. Don't think that's wrong. In fact, it's usually after a light rain on a sunny day versus a heavy downpour on a dark day. You can also see rainbows in mist or fog. Go look at a waterfall sometime where the mist is coming off the water and the light is shining through. Chances are you'll see a rainbow if you look long enough and find the right angle. You just need the light to bend in the right way off the water.

The takeaway: Keep an eye out for rainbows after light rains, around waterfalls, in mist, or even in fog. Don't forget to take a picture.

Additional facts: Have you ever heard of a lunar rainbow? It's when light reflects off the moon's surface and creates a rainbow in the sky. They aren't always easy to see (they often look white), but try to take notice in the sky on a clear night and see if you can see a rainbow coming from the moon.

8: When gardening, you can't mix sun and shade plants.

MYTH SCALE: 2

About the myth: If you look on a plant's label, you'll see that it has specific light needs. Usually it'll say full-sun, part-sun, part-shade, or full-shade. So it seems like it would make sense not to mix any of these together, right?

The truth: If you're reading the label on the plants you buy, then you should be proud of yourself! A lot of people don't even read the labels, and then they plant flowers in places where they never even stand a chance. But even the label has a little wiggle room. Just because a plant needs sun doesn't mean it can't have any shade at all and vice versa. Some shade plants can tolerate sun as well.

The takeaway: While you probably don't want to mix too many full-sun and full-shade plants, you can still mix those part-sun or part-shade ones. One of the best ways to do this is with a container. This way, you can move the container around a bit so it gets a nice mix of both sun and shade. So use plant labels as a guide, but don't take them too seriously.

Additional facts: Some traditional shade plants like coleus or impatiens are now being adapted to have a sun version as well. Most vegetables need lots of sun too. But if you don't have a ton of sun in your backyard, try growing lettuce. It will tolerate a lot more shade.

Be a Scientist

EXPERIMENT WITH GROWING SEEDS

It's fun to grow your own fruits, vegetables, and flowers. But before they become pretty or ready to eat, they're just tiny little seeds. Which seeds sprout first? Which ones are easiest to grow? Time to experiment!

Supplies: Seeds, soil, containers, a light source
Time: 20 minutes planting time; a few days to a couple weeks to get sprouts
Observe and learn: Keep a journal to write down or draw pictures of which seeds sprout first. You might also set up some seeds under natural light and some under lightbulbs to see how that affects the sprouting.

How-To:

1. Pick out the seeds you want to grow. Your local garden center will carry seeds year-round, so you can try this activity anytime. Pick out a few different veggies so you can compare.
2. Prepare your containers with a good soil mixture. You can use old plastic bins or even cardboard boxes for this experiment.
3. Plant the seeds according to the instructions on the back of the seed packet.
4. Place containers in a mixture of natural sunlight and indoor lighting. You'll want to make sure the containers are in a warm location. If it's too cold, the seeds won't sprout.
5. Check on your seeds every few days and make notes on which ones sprouted first, second, third, etc. If it's the right season to transfer seeds outside, plant them and watch them grow. Otherwise, you could repeat this experiment and alter the growing conditions to see what difference it makes.

Pick up a grow bulb at your garden center for less than $5. You can place it in an ordinary lamp to create an ideal growing space.

9: If you cut a worm in half, you'll grow two worms.
MYTH SCALE: 2

About the myth: This myth has been around for decades. Some places suggest that worm heads and tails are exactly the same, so even if you cut a worm in half, it'll grow a new half and will survive as two separate worms. But hold on there before you try this experiment for yourself.

The truth: Worm heads and tails are not exactly the same. So if you cut a worm in half, the tail will usually die. The head, however, might or might not be able to grow a new tail. It depends on how far up you cut it and its overall ability to regrow. By the way, this ability to regrow is called regeneration. Earthworms are known for being able to regenerate lost segments, for example, if a bird ate a piece out of its tail.

The takeaway: You probably shouldn't even try this experiment for yourself. If you cut a worm in half, you should just assume it's going to die because there's a good chance it will. And almost certainly, half of it will.

Additional facts: Want to know the easiest way to tell a worm's head from its tail? You put it out in the open and see which way it starts to crawl first. Worms usually crawl headfirst.

Weather Legends

MARCH COMES IN LIKE A LION AND GOES OUT LIKE A LAMB.

For much of the United States, March is a transition month weatherwise. Late winter lingers on, while the early-spring days tease the nice weather that is just around the corner. This legend won't hold up every year, but it does ring true sometimes.

10: Bees die after they sting you.

MYTH SCALE: 2

About the myth: No one likes to get stung by a bee—ouch! But isn't it just a little bit satisfying to know bees are done after stinging you once? Then they'll never sting anyone again! Well, that's how the myth goes at least.

The truth: Yes, this myth is partly true, because honeybees can only sting once. This is because when their stinger goes into your skin, they can't pull it back out again without ripping out part of their abdomen. Ouch for you and them! So they die shortly after. Honeybees are not the only bees out there though. There are about 20,000 different species of bees in the world, and many bees can sting you over and over and over again.

The takeaway: It's true that honeybees can only sting you once, but all the other bees out there, including bumblebees, can sting you multiple times. So can wasps and hornets. Most insects won't bother you unless they feel threatened though. Leave them alone, and chances are they'll leave you alone too.

Additional facts: Another bee-related myth is that bumblebees can't sting at all. This is not true. They can sting but rarely do. Just leave them alone, and you shouldn't have to worry about them. Instead, enjoy watching them fly around your flowers.

11: Snakes can't hear because they don't have ears.

MYTH SCALE: 3

About the myth: Snakes don't have outer ears like many traditional animals, so for years scientists thought that they couldn't hear at all. They believed snakes used their other senses to get information about their surroundings. Then scientists who study reptiles (called herpetologists) started learning new things.

The truth: Snakes do have inner ears. You just can't see them. But how does the noise travel to the inner ear? Scientists think that the sound travels there through the jawbone! The way their jaw moves from side to side makes it possible for sound to transfer up to their inner ears.

The takeaway: Snakes can hear even though they don't have distinct outer ears. Maybe this means you shouldn't go sneaking up on a snake!

Additional facts: Here's another fun fact about snakes and their senses—they can actually use their tongues to smell things! You know how snakes stick out their tongues a lot? Turns out there are reasons they are doing this. They're using their tongue to help them gather important information about their surroundings.

12: All plants are grown from seeds.

MYTH SCALE: 1

About the myth: Ahh, springtime! This means it's growing season, so you can go to your local garden center and gather up all kinds of new plants to grow in your backyard. You can hit the seed aisle to sow your own seeds, or you can buy plants that someone else already started from seeds. And those are the only two ways to garden, right?

The truth: Seeds are a very common way to grow plants, but they aren't the only way! Think about the tulips and daffodils that you see popping up in spring—those aren't grown from seeds! Nope, they're grown from bulbs that you plant in the ground in fall. Here's another tricky one: potatoes. To grow potatoes, you plant a piece of potato in the spring, making sure it has a good "eye" where the plant can come out of. Both of these are exceptions to the seed rule.

The takeaway: Seeds are definitely the most common and cheap way to grow plants, but they aren't the only way. If it's springtime, pick up some iris rhizomes to plant for summer blooms or some potato eyes so you'll get a nice summer harvest.

Additional facts: Another way people like to grow plants is by taking a cutting. You just take a snip of a leaf or even a branch in some instances (like with red-twig dogwood) and stick it in some soil. In the right conditions and with a little practice, you can grow a whole new plant!

ASPARAGUS CAN MAKE YOUR PEE SMELL.

Have you ever tried asparagus? It is one of the earliest spring vegetables, popping up as the ground thaws. This is a yummy veggie that grows as tall, thin stalks. It looks like a green pencil with a little crown on top. The coolest thing about asparagus isn't its fresh taste though. Asparagus contains asparagusic acid. It sounds a little weird, but it's just a compound that is high in sulfur.

So what does this mean? When this breaks down in the body, it can make your pee smell really odd. Here is the real kicker though: Less than 50 percent of people get this. In fact, it's still kind of a mystery. Do certain people just not get this, or do they lack the right receptors to smell it? You kind of want to test it for yourself now, don't you?

Asparagus take two years to establish in the garden. You can't get a harvest out of it the first year, but after that it will come back year after year.

13: April showers bring May flowers.

MYTH SCALE: 2

About the myth: This has been a popular saying for years. It has to do with the spring rainy season. April tends to be a month with lots of rainfall, which in turn helps lead to gorgeous flowers in May.

The truth: Rain definitely leads to healthy flowers throughout the year, but you don't have to have showers in April to have flowers in May. It might happen this way sometimes, but it doesn't have to be the rule. February or March showers can lead to great flowers in other parts of the country. Other areas might have hardly any rain at all, but they'll still get great flowers.

The takeaway: While sayings like these are fun and usually have a little bit of truth to them, they aren't always true. Remember that April in one part of the country can be different than another. For example, southern Arizona and northern Minnesota have very different types of April weather.

Additional facts: April can also bring late frosts, so you have to be a little bit careful when you add new plants to your garden. Most instructions will say, "Plant after the danger of frost has passed." For most people, it's safe to plant by mid- to late April, but others have to wait until the end of May!

Stranger than Fiction

A LIGHTNING BOLT IS HOTTER THAN THE SUN'S SURFACE.

It happens so fast you might not think about lightning as being a big heat source. But it is. Lightning is actually a discharge of sorts of an electrical charge. And it is hot. Hotter than pizza right out of the oven. Hotter than lava spewing from a volcano. Even hotter than the surface of the sun.

While the core sun temperature can reach a scorching 15 million kelvins (which is about 27 million degrees Fahrenheit), the temperature on the surface of the sun is merely 6,000 kelvins (around 10,340 degrees Fahrenheit). Lightning can be upward of 30,000 kelvins (greater than 53,500 degrees Fahrenheit) by comparison.

How is lightning formed? Water molecules bump into each other within the cloud. This creates electrical charges with the positive charges (protons) forming at the top of the cloud and the negative charges (electrons) at the bottom of the cloud. Lightning happens when the negative charges meet up with positive charges. This can happen in the cloud or with charges on the ground.

14: Turkeys will drown in the rain.

MYTH SCALE: 3

About the myth: This is a pretty funny myth when you think about it. The way it's told is that turkeys are so dumb that when it rains, they stare up into the sky with their mouths hanging open because they are so mesmerized. Pretty soon the rain starts to collect and the turkeys eventually drown.

The truth: Turkeys aren't necessarily dumb. They have what is called monocular vision because their eyes are on either side of their heads. This allows them to look at two things at once, but they can't focus on just one single object like we humans do. Scientists have observed turkeys staring into the sky on occasion, but it's a genetic behavior and has nothing to do with rain.

The takeaway: Turkeys might tilt their heads one way or another to get a good look at something, but they are not so dumb that they will drown in the rain.

Additional facts: While the bald eagle is now the national bird, it almost wasn't. Benjamin Franklin wanted the wild turkey to be our national bird symbol.

MAKE YOUR OWN RAIN GAUGE

Bring on those raindrops! You can test your meteorologist skills by measuring the rain in your backyard with your very own rain gauge. All you really need to get started is to look in the recycling bin.

Supplies: Clear recycled jar, markers, ruler
Time: 30 minutes
Observe and learn: Use this project to learn more about the weather. Go to weather websites to find out when rain is in the forecast, and then see how your predictions match up with theirs.

How-To:

1. Look for that perfect jar in the recycling bin. Best-case scenario: It is clear and the bottom of the jar and the top of the jar are about the same width. This will help ensure you have more accurate measurements. Remove any labels on the jar, and clean it.
2. Use a ruler to carefully mark different measurements on your jar. You'll probably want to mark at least every ¼ inch. Make sure you use a permanent marker so your marks don't come off in the rain.
3. After you have your measurements marked, decorate and personalize your jar.
4. Find a place outside to place your jar. You'll want to make sure the location is flat and out in the open. If you place it under a tree, you won't get accurate measurements.

5. Now all you can do is wait! Check and record the rain in your jar every few days or sooner if you're getting a lot of rain. Try to make a goal of recording the rain in your area for an entire month before you dump the jar and start over. Another option is to dump the rain gauge out after every rain so you can keep track of the different storms.

"Meteorologist" is a fancy word for someone who studies the weather.

The rain gauge we know today was created more than one hundred years ago, but reports in history show humans have been finding ways to measure rain since the 1400s!

A SAGUARO CACTUS DOESN'T GROW ARMS FOR FIFTY YEARS.

The saguaro cactus is an icon of the Sonoran Desert. These towering giants are basically the forests of the region. But they might not always look how you think they do. You know how cacti are often shown having three distinct arms? For many years the saguaro lacks these altogether. They actually grow slowly, and they don't start to branch for fifty to seventy years. In drier locations it can take as long as one hundred years before arms start to appear.

If you ever get the chance to look at a saguaro cactus up close, you should. They look round, but if you examine them closely, you'll see that they have many pleats that can swell open and closed like an accordion as the cactus stores up water.

The average life span for a saguaro cactus is between 150 and 175 years. A large cactus can be over 50 feet tall and can weigh over 6 tons.

15: To live underwater requires gills.

MYTH SCALE: 2

About the myth: It's common knowledge that fish have gills. In fact, it's those gills that allow them to live and breathe underwater. So it must be common for other animals that live underwater to have gills as well, right? Not so fast!

The truth: Lots of animals live underwater without having gills. To start with, dolphins and whales don't have gills at all. They both have lungs and blowholes. They can stay underwater for long periods of time. Then they come to the surface to breathe in new air through the blowholes on the tops of their bodies. Another underwater creature that doesn't have gills is the frog. Several species of frogs live around and under water, yet they come to the surface to breathe as well.

The takeaway: Fish definitely have gills and need them to breathe underwater, but there are actually lots of other animals that can live in oceans and lakes that do not breathe in this way. In general, water animals are fascinating. Get a good nonfiction book from the library about animals that live in water. Learn which ones have gills and which ones don't. You might be surprised!

Additional facts: There are some pretty impressive animals that can stay under the water a long time without having to come to the surface to breathe. For example, the hippopotamus stays underwater for 5, 15, or even 30 minutes at a time. Sea turtles can stay underwater for up to 5 hours if they need to. And some species of whales can stay under the water for a couple of hours!

16: Rainbows have seven colors.

MYTH SCALE: 1

About the myth: At a very young age, kids learn the seven colors of the rainbow using the acronym ROY G BIV. The letters stand for red, orange, yellow, green, blue, indigo, and violet. Millions of kids have been learning about rainbows in this way for decades. How can they all be wrong?

The truth: Here's the thing: Yes, rainbows will often have seven colors. But did you know they actually have lots of other colors that the human eye just can't see? In addition, even though we can see those seven colors, they don't always line up perfectly for everyone. Every once in a while, you have that perfect rainbow with the seven distinct colors. But more often than not, you might see five colors or colors that look a little different than the standard ones of ROY G BIV.

The takeaway: There are many factors that go into making a rainbow. You might see a perfect rainbow with seven colors one day and then a gorgeous five-color rainbow another day. Plus, there are those rainbows with dozens and dozens of colors that we just can't see at all. The next time you see a rainbow, look closely to see how many colors you can spot.

Additional facts: Here's another fun little trick about rainbows: Whenever you see a rainbow, take a minute to notice how the sun is always behind you. The center of the rainbow is also situated in the direction opposite the sun. This has to do with the way the light has to shine in order to see a rainbow. Test it out!

17: Male mosquitoes don't buzz.

MYTH SCALE: 3

About the myth: *Bzzz, bzzz, bzzz.* You know that annoying *bzzz* around your ear? It's like the mosquito is just hanging out there, teasing you and waiting to swoop in and bite you. Is it really a female mosquito? Are they really the only ones that *bzzz*?

The truth: It's pretty silly to think only females have a *bzzz* sound. This is not true at all. However, the females are probably the ones buzzing around your ear, and here's why: Only female mosquitoes can bite. They need your blood for protein for their eggs, while the males feed on flower nectar instead.

The takeaway: While both males and females buzz, the females are the ones to blame for biting you. Don't think you can get away from them though. Mosquitoes can detect you from far away just based on your breathing.

Additional facts: Believe it or not, they say mosquitoes are one of the most deadly animals in the world. This sounds pretty strange, right? It's not because they are all that dangerous by themselves, but they carry a lot of diseases like malaria, yellow fever, and other diseases that can lead to death.

Weather Legends

IF YOU STICK A KNIFE IN THE GROUND, IT WON'T RAIN.

This is especially a popular test for brides to try on their wedding day. A lot of brides don't want it to rain on the day they are getting married, although other people will claim it's good luck. Either way, it's something people have been trying for generations.

18: Eating spinach makes you stronger.

MYTH SCALE: 2

About the myth: A lot of people think Popeye is the one that got this myth started. Popeye was a cartoon character in the 1920s, and whenever he would eat spinach, he would immediately get strong so he could go and save the day. This helped give parents and grandparents a new reason to try to get their kids to eat this leafy green.

The truth: First of all, this myth goes back a lot earlier than Popeye. The way the story goes is that back in the 1870s, a scientist said that spinach contained up to ten times more iron than other green veggies. This wasn't actually true, but it's probably the reason this myth got started in the first place. Second of all, spinach isn't necessarily healthier than other leafy greens.

The takeaway: A good rule of thumb is that you shouldn't believe anything that promises immediate results. Spinach is a very healthy vegetable and gives you lots of great health benefits, but eating it will not make you stronger on its own.

Additional facts: Spinach is also known for being a good source of vitamin C and vitamin A. It's a cool-season crop, which means it's a great one to plant in spring. Then harvest spinach before it gets too big—the leaves are best when they're smaller.

Weather Legends

IF YOU SEE A RAINBOW IN THE MORNING, IT'S GOING TO RAIN LATER THAT DAY.

Yes, rainbows are often associated with rain, so this isn't a terrible predictor. But it doesn't necessarily count as an indicator. Do a little testing and see if this one holds up for you.

19: Milk only comes from cows.

MYTH SCALE: 2

About the myth: Milk does a body good, right? Milk contains vitamin D, which helps your bones grow nice and strong. And everyone knows that milk comes from cows. It's one of the basic things you learn as a kid.

The truth: The majority of milk around the world does come from cows, but it's not the only source. Goats are another source of milk, and many people prefer the flavor of goat milk to cow milk. Another source of milk (which some people say isn't real milk) is soybeans. Soy milk is popular for people who are lactose intolerant. This means their bodies can't process dairy products as well, so they have to have alternatives like soy milk to eat their cereal. It's not a true milk product because it comes from beans instead of an animal, but it's still a great source for lots of people.

The takeaway: Milk really does do a body good, but cows aren't the only source. Go out and see if you can find a milk alternative to see how it compares to the cow milk that you're used to.

Additional facts: Milk is a great source of vitamin D, but there's another source to get this essential vitamin. Just go outside! Just a few hours of sunshine will give you the vitamin D you need as well. This doesn't mean you still shouldn't drink your milk though. It gives you other great vitamins as well.

20: Bees gather honey from flowers.

MYTH SCALE: 3

About the myth: We all know that bees are associated with honey in some way, right? We also know that bees go to flowers to dig out something sweet, right? Well, if you put the two together, then it's easy to think that bees are gathering honey straight from the flower and then taking it back to their hives.

The truth: Bees are not gathering honey straight from flowers. They are actually gathering nectar. Nectar in flowers is like a sugar water, mostly made up of water. But the process of making honey is just getting started. Worker bees store this sugar water in their stomachs and then regurgitate it to a hive bee back at the hive. It continues to break down in the hive bee's stomach. Next it is regurgitated and stored in the hive's honeycomb.

The takeaway: This process is a bit more complicated than it sounds, but the main thing to remember is that bees are not gathering honey from flowers. They are gathering sugar water. The honey part comes later.

Additional facts: While the bees gather the nectar, they are also pollinating the flowers because they are transferring pollen grain from one flower to the next. This is really important for flowers. They need to be pollinated to grow nice and healthy. So it's okay to be cautious of bees, but don't be afraid. You should encourage them to be in your backyard!

BIRDS CAN HAVE ACCENTS.

Accents can be heard all over the world. They are just different regional dialects that people have. For instance, people from the South say certain words differently than people in the Northeast. And people from one area of the country might have a different twang or tone than another part. Well, this is fine and dandy, but everybody knows birds say "tweet," right? How can one tweet be that different from another one? It turns out birds can speak with accents too.

Birds of different species all sing different songs. But for some, like the white-crowned sparrow, these songs vary slightly from one part of the country to another. Some birds automatically know how to sing their species song. Others learn it by listening to their parents or neighboring birds. But this is a pretty fun one to put to the test for yourself. Listen to the birds in your area, and then when you're on vacation or otherwise visiting another part of the country, listen to the birds there too.

There are some reports that cows also have different accents—that cows moo differently in different locations—but there seems to be less evidence to support this theory.

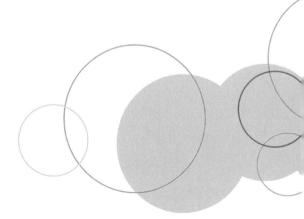

21: You'll catch more fish right before it rains.
MYTH SCALE: 2

About the myth: This particular myth is told in many different ways. Some say you catch more fish right before it rains. Others say you catch more fish right after it rains. Some people say you catch more fish on a cloudy day, while others say you'll have better luck on sunny days. So what's the deal with all these fishing myths? When are you supposed to go out fishing for the best results?

The truth: Everyone who is good at fishing seems to have his or her own methods or beliefs for how to catch fish. What works for one person doesn't necessarily work for someone else though. It could be that what works in one pond, lake, or river doesn't really work at another.

The takeaway: Here's a great excuse to do a little experimenting. While you can't say for sure that you will always catch more fish before it rains, it's worth testing out the theory. Get out a notebook and make a little chart. Fish in all kinds of conditions—sunny, cloudy, rainy, before rain, after rain, morning, evening—and see what works best.

Additional facts: Have you also heard that you should be quiet when fishing so the fish don't hear you? This is somewhat true. You don't need to whisper, but you shouldn't be yelling and splashing about where you're trying to fish because this could scare the fish away.

Luck Legends

IF THE FIRST BUTTERFLY YOU SEE IN SPRING IS WHITE, YOU'LL HAVE GOOD LUCK.

There is a family of butterflies called the Whites and a closely related family called the Sulphurs. Both are light colored. If you are on the lookout for white butterflies, the cabbage white is one of the earliest species you could spot in spring. You can find it throughout much of North America.

22: Tornados turn clockwise.

MYTH SCALE: 2

About the myth: When you think of something spinning, chances are you imagine it spinning clockwise, right? We are all accustomed to seeing this direction, so it makes sense that tornadoes would follow this pattern as well.

The truth: Most tornadoes rotate counterclockwise north of the equator and clockwise south of the equator. But tornadoes are unpredictable and don't always follow the rules. They've been seen turning both ways.

The takeaway: This is one myth that you probably shouldn't try to see for yourself. Tornadoes are very destructive, and it's not safe to try to get a close look at them. You can watch videos of tornadoes though. See if you can tell if the funnel spins in one direction or the other.

Additional facts: Don't think size makes a difference when it comes to tornadoes. Just because there's a big tornado doesn't mean it's more dangerous or destructive than smaller ones. In fact, small tornadoes have been known to do even more damage in a lot of cases.

23: Fish either live in freshwater or in salt water.

MYTH SCALE: 2

About the myth: If you have pet fish, then you know that you either have a freshwater tank or a saltwater tank, but you can't mix them. Many of those beautiful tropical fish you see at the fish store need a special saltwater tank. So it should be the same for fish in the wild, right?

The truth: It's true that in many cases, fish either live in fresh or salt water. For instance, catfish and bass tend to be freshwater lake fish, while marlins and swordfish are in oceans (salt water). There are fish that will cross between freshwater and salt water though. They are called euryhaline species and can adapt to many conditions. For instance, salmon are born in freshwater but spend most of their lives in salt water. They just return to freshwater when they spawn (when they go to lay their eggs). In other examples, some fish spend most of their time in freshwater but then go to salt water to spawn. This is the case with eels.

The takeaway: Most fish don't go back and forth between freshwater and salt water because they can't survive very well, but there are a few exceptions to the rule.

Additional facts: While most bass are freshwater fish, there is one exception to this too. Striped bass are found along the Atlantic coast-line, and they will go between freshwater and salt water.

SOME ANIMALS EAT THEIR BABIES' POOP.

Why would anything eat poop? It sounds gross, but there is a logical reason. Some animals do it to save their babies. For instance, many songbird hatchlings deposit fecal sacs. (This is like a little sac of the waste.) The parents either remove or consume these in an effort to protect the nests and young from detection by predators. Similarly, some mammal parents will also eat the waste from their young to help keep them safe.

While we are on the topic of poop eating, did you know that rabbits and a few other critters consume their own feces as a way to get added nutrients? They don't digest their food that well initially, so they eat it twice. Then they'll poop out the waste the second time around.

"Coprophagia" is the technical term for eating poop. It doesn't make it sound any better though.

CATFISH HAVE MORE TASTE BUDS THAN HUMANS.

Catfish live in some of the dankest, darkest, murkiest waters. They like it when it's muddy, and it can be hard to see anything else in the water. They are very interesting fish, and one of the most amazing facts about them has to do with their taste buds. People have about 10,000 taste buds, and all of these are conveniently located in the mouth. By comparison, catfish have taste buds over much of their bodies. They are most dense along the "whiskers," but overall, they can have upward of 250,000 taste buds. Wow! Can you imagine tasting things if all of your skin was like a giant tongue?

Catfish have other senses that are well developed too. There was even research into using catfish as early-warning detectors for predicting earthquakes because they are sensitive to low-frequency vibrations.

24: Place butter on a burn to soothe the pain.

MYTH SCALE: 3

About the myth: No one likes to get burned! Burns can sting for several days, so if you can do something to reduce the pain (even a little bit), then you'll definitely want to. This myth has been around for decades. The way it supposedly works is that if you put butter on a burn right away, it'll help soothe the pain and keep it from getting infected.

The truth: Over the years there have been all kinds of quirky methods suggested for soothing burns. Butter and even egg whites are a couple of the methods, but you probably shouldn't practice either one of these because they could do more harm than good. Putting things on open skin could actually lead to an infection, so it's probably best to leave applying any type of medication to a doctor.

The takeaway: Before you reach into the refrigerator, you should probably find a different method to sooth burns. And really, it's best to leave medical advice up to a medical professional.

Additional facts: A lot of people think you should apply ice to a burn, but this isn't the case either. If you have just a small, minor burn, you should run it under cold water instead.

Be a Scientist

CREATE A RAINBOW

A rainbow is always a welcome sight to see in the sky, but did you know you could also create your own indoors? With the right lighting and just a few ordinary objects, you could create a whole wall of rainbows.

Supplies: Compact disc (CD), glass of water, flashlight, white piece of paper
Time: 10 minutes
Observe and learn: Notice how the rainbow forms only when you have the right reflection of light. Try different angles and positions to see how to make the best rainbow.

How-To:

1. There are two really easy ways to make a rainbow. For the first way, take an old CD and make sure the surface is nice and clean.
2. Next, hold the CD up to a source of light. If it's a sunny day, you should be able to catch the sunshine coming in from a window. Play with the placement of the CD a little bit until you get the right angle. Once you get it right, you should see a rainbow bouncing off a nearby wall, the ceiling, or the floor.
3. Now try this next way of making a rainbow with a glass of water about three-quarters of the way full. Again, you'll need to find a sunny window.
4. Place a white piece of paper on the floor where the sun is shining in and then hold your glass of water above the paper. You might have to play with the placement a bit again. Pretty soon you should see the sunlight going through the glass to create a rainbow on your piece of paper.
5. If you don't have a sunny day, you can still try these experiments using a flashlight. Try replicating sunshine with your flashlight. If you can't seem to create a rainbow, cover part of your flashlight with tape so you're working with a smaller space. Then keep practicing. Once you get it down, you can create a whole roomful of rainbows as long as you have a few friends around to help you.

You can also buy a prism to help you create a rainbow. Prisms are glass or plastic that bend or refract light.

25: Bulls will attack the color red.

MYTH SCALE: 2

About the myth: You've seen the images of bullfighters waving a red cape, taunting a bull into attacking, then sidestepping away from harm. Does this make you afraid to walk past cattle while wearing a red shirt? What is it about the color red? Orange is similar to red, so will that have the same effect?

The truth: For the most part, cattle are pretty calm critters. Generally they are going to mind their own business. The most exciting part of their day could be chewing on their cud. The flip side of that is that like most animals, cattle might chase after something that is harassing them. As for the color red being the cue, cattle lack the receptors to even see the color red. They aren't colorblind, but their eyes can't pick out reds. Blues and yellows are most visible to them.

The takeaway: Both males (bulls) and females (cows) can be feisty at times. Cows can be especially protective of their calves. A few breeds tend to be more assertive than others, but cattle aren't especially aggressive, and they won't attack red. So next time you visit a farm, feel free to wear a red shirt.

Additional facts: Bullfighting using a red cape has been a long-standing tradition in many countries, including Spain and Portugal, and this is the reason people think bulls will attack the color red. Remember, though, that they are trained to do this.

26: All rivers flow south.

MYTH SCALE: 2

About the myth: If the equator is in the middle of the earth, then shouldn't the rivers in North America flow south toward it? A lot of people think this makes sense, and they think of things going from north to south naturally.

The truth: The fact of the matter is that lots of rivers don't flow south. Sure, lots of rivers in North America do flow south, but many flow east and west too. And there are many that flow north too.

The takeaway: You can't assume things will travel in a direction like west to east, north to south, and so on. When it comes to the natural world, there are very few rules!

Additional facts: One of the most famous rivers in the whole world flows north. Do you know which one it is? It's the Nile! The Nile River is in Egypt and is more than 4,000 miles long.

27: Pigs can't look up.

MYTH SCALE: 2

About the myth: Think about a pig for a second and the way its body is structured. It has a long body and short stubby legs. In fact, it almost looks like it has no neck at all. So what does a pig do when it's trying to look up anyway? How can it stretch its neck back that far?

The truth: It might not seem like pigs can stretch their necks back and look up into the sky, but they are pretty smart animals. First of all, they can actually look up. Perhaps they aren't able to stretch their necks back as far as other animals, but they can still look up a little bit. Second of all, since they're so smart, they would find a way to look up if they wanted to. For instance, they could put their little hooves up on something and stretch back this way to get a better angle.

The takeaway: If a pig wants to find a way to look up and see something, it will. But sometimes you have to see it to believe it. Check out a pig if you can sometime, and watch its behavior. You'll probably see that it can look up, and that it's pretty smart too.

Additional facts: The phrase "sweat like a pig" means you are sweating a lot. This isn't related to pigs at all but rather to pig iron. Pigs don't sweat at all because they don't have those glands. To cool off, they will hang out in the cool mud instead. During the formation of pig iron, the iron "sweats" as it cools off.

28: You can start a fire by rubbing two sticks together.

MYTH SCALE: 2

About the myth: If you're out in the wild and need to start a fire, all you need is a couple of sticks. At least that's how the myth goes. You rub those two sticks together and the friction this creates will get a few sparks going, which will in turn get a fire going. This has been demonstrated in all kinds of cartoons, so it must be pretty easy, right?

The truth: It's a little unclear where this myth actually started, but it is very difficult, if not impossible, to start a fire with just two sticks. Go ahead and give it a try yourself. Find a couple of sticks in the woods and start rubbing them together. Chances are you're going to give up long before you create any amount of friction or even smoke. If you're going camping, you should make sure you pack matches or a lighter.

The takeaway: You should probably just leave the sticks in the fire instead of trying to rub them together to try to create one. Yes, it might not be impossible altogether, but the chance of making fire this way is slim.

Additional facts: A challenging but much easier way to make fire without using matches is to use flint. If you can learn the right way to strike flint, you can create sparks and start a fire.

Weather Legends

IF A SPIDER SPINS ITS WEB BEFORE NOON, THEN SUNNY WEATHER WILL FOLLOW.

If you believe this one, then you're probably looking around for spiders in hopes of sunshine! Don't count on it, though. There are many spiders out there that don't even build webs (did you notice that myth?). Another popular myth related to spiders and weather is that they build thicker webs when the weather turns cold.

29: A rooster only crows in the morning.

MYTH SCALE: 3

About the myth: Here's how the story goes. It's early in the morning in the farmyard, and the sun is just starting to peek out above the horizon. The rooster struts out of the chicken coop, raises his head to the sky, and lets out a loud *cock-a-doodle-doo*. The farmer wakes up and then goes about his day on the farm. So is this a real scenario? Does it really happen?

The truth: It doesn't matter what time of day it is—morning, noon, or night—roosters are going to crow whenever they feel like it. If there are two roosters in an area, they're going to crow even more. This is because they do so, in part, to claim their territory.

The takeaway: Roosters are not crowing in the morning to wake people up. Well, they do often wake people up in the morning with their crowing, but it's not deliberate. They will crow all day long, so if they happen to be crowing more in the morning, it's just a coincidence.

Additional facts: Roosters are just boy chickens, but most people know this already. Did you also know that roosters and chickens can fly? They can't fly far because they have pretty heavy bodies, but they *can* fly!

30: In North America, earthquakes occur mostly in California.

MYTH SCALE: 2

About the myth: When people think of earthquakes in the United States, they usually think of California. Have you heard about how California is going to fall into the ocean one day? Well, that's not actually true, and neither is this myth. Learn a little bit more about why.

The truth: California is along the zone where most earthquakes occur. The zone is pretty big, though, and doesn't just cover California. It also goes along the South American coast, Central America, and Mexico and extends around to other parts of the world as well. This area is called the Ring of Fire. Yes, California experiences lots of earthquakes, but Alaska gets even more!

The takeaway: Earthquakes don't just happen in California. You just hear about the ones in California a lot more because they affect a lot more people and buildings. Oftentimes, the ones in Alaska happen where nothing else is around.

Additional facts: Earthquakes aren't just on the West Coast either. They can occur anywhere in North America. They might not be as strong as the earthquakes in California or along the Ring of Fire, but you can still get them anywhere.

31: All spiders make webs to catch food.

MYTH SCALE: 2

About the myth: What makes a spider a spider? It's the ability to make a spiderweb, right? It just makes sense that all spiders know how to make webs. How can you be a spider if you can't make a web?

The truth: Scientists are still learning lots about spiders. There are over 40,000 described species, but they say the actual number could be three to five times higher. There are numerous styles of spiderwebs out there too. But the bottom line is, not all spiders build webs. While we think of many spiders using webs to catch food, spider silk can serve many other functions too. Spiders can also wrap their prey up mummy-style with their silk without needing a web at all. They can also use it to line burrows where they live or make egg sacks.

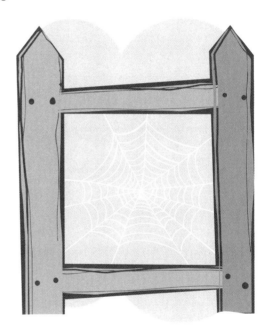

The takeaway: Even though not all spiders make webs, they can be an effective way for spiders to catch food. But it isn't the only way. Many species, especially jumping spiders, fishing spiders, and wolf spiders, stalk their prey. They don't need webs and instead sneak up on their meals. Other spiders wait for their dinner to come to them. Crab spiders, for example, sit camouflaged on flowers, snapping up unsuspecting insects as they pass by.

Additional facts: Spiders use spider silk for one more thing called ballooning. Ballooning is like a hot-air balloon ride for young spiders as they relocate to new areas.

Stranger than Fiction

YOU CAN EAT FLOWERS.

How many times have you heard that you should eat your fruits and veggies? Well, now you can also add flowers to that list. It's true. Don't be afraid to try it. There are many species of flowers that are not just edible, they are plumb tasty.

We eat many different plant parts already, so it should come as no surprise that many flowers are also edible. But remember that not all plants are safe to eat, and neither are all flowers. If you are looking to try some flowers, you could start with shooting stars. They often come straight out of a mountain meadow and have a lovely subtle radish flavor. Pansies are also a good flower to try eating and add a touch of color and charm to fresh salads.

Dandelions are another flower you can eat. Use the leaves and young flowers. Once the blooms get bigger, they are pretty bitter.

32: Turtles have teeth.

MYTH SCALE: 3

About the myth: Turtles have sharp teeth and can bite a broom handle right in half. They also have an egg tooth when they are born to help them break out of the egg, so turtles must have teeth, right?

The truth: The bite of a turtle can be something fierce, and a couple of species of turtles might be able to put a hurting on a broom, but turtles don't have teeth! Some species of turtle have a diet heavy in meat and live animals. They don't need teeth though. A turtle mouth is sometimes referred to as a beak. The turtle beak has sharp ridges and bony plates to help grasp prey and tear off bits of meat. As far as the egg tooth goes, this

is partially true. However, it isn't a real tooth. This structure is more like a miniature rhino horn. Baby turtles use this egg tooth to bust out of their shells, and then it falls off shortly after hatching.

The takeaway: Turtles don't have teeth, but this doesn't mean they can't bite! The mouths of turtles are quite varied from one species to the next. Yes, some have sharp edges, but none have teeth.

Additional facts: If you look at the fossils of some turtle species that are now extinct, you can see that many did have teeth.

33: A snail is a slug with a shell on its back.

MYTH SCALE: 3

About the myth: Snails and slugs look pretty much exactly alike. They seem like they are pretty much the same thing. Do you think a slug could find a shell, crawl up inside, and turn into snail? Or if a snail gets tired of hauling around a bulky shell, could it set off for the freestyle life of a slug?

The truth: They look like the same thing, but they're not. There are numerous species of both snails and slugs. Most are aquatic (live in water). Others are terrestrial (live on land). The terrestrial ones secrete slimy mucus. This helps them slide along. It also helps them retain moisture so they don't shrivel up and die. As long as nobody pours salt on them, snails and slugs can live up to twenty-five years in the wild.

A fundamental difference between snails and slugs is the shell, so let's focus on it. Snail shell formation is a pretty complicated process. The snails are born with their shells, although it isn't quite the full shell you're picturing. The shell continues to grow throughout the lifetime of the snail. Both snails and slugs need to maintain a certain amount of dampness about them. In addition to secreting mucus, they tend to hang out in cool, moist environments.

The takeaway: Snails and slugs are related to each other. Despite many similarities though, no matter how hard they try, slugs will never become snails. And snails will never become slugs. They'll always be different critters. Both are considered mollusks, but so are octopuses, squids, clams, and oysters.

Additional facts: Snails and slugs are both known as gastropods, a term that combines the Greek words for stomach (*gastros*) and foot (*podos*). There are also species of gastropods known as semislugs. These have reduced shells that are usually softer than the shells of true snails.

BUTTERFLIES TASTE WITH THEIR FEET.

It's interesting to watch those lovely butterflies flitting about from flower to flower. They'll gently land, stamp their feet a few times, and then either flick out their crazy long proboscis (this is a fancy word for tongue) or flutter on by.

Remember butterflies don't really have mouthparts like people do. Instead of biting and chewing, they slurp nutrients up through their proboscis. Butterflies aren't just there to taste what is on the menu either. They will use other parts of their body, including their feet, to help detect the proper host plants on which to lay their eggs. They have sensors on their feet to help with this. Host plants are really important because caterpillars often rely on specific plants on which to feed and attach. So they have to make sure to get it right when laying their eggs. It's a good thing they have unique feet to help them do this!

Here's another interesting fact about butterflies and their senses: Butterflies use their antennae to smell.

34: If you lay a rope around your campsite at night, snakes will not crawl in.

MYTH SCALE: 3

About the myth: This myth seems to make the rounds with all back-packers and cowboys. The thought is that the snake won't crawl over the rope. One version of the myth is that you must use a horsehair rope. The theory here is that this rope is rough, so it will scratch the snake.

The truth: Snakes aren't going to come into your camp, unzip your tent, and slither into your sleeping bag at night. And putting a rope out wouldn't be an effective barrier anyway. Snakes slither up and over all kinds of things. Some snakes spend a fair bit of time in the trees, while others rarely venture out from under rocks or leaves. But any of them could crawl over a rope easy enough.

The takeaway: Snakes are really cool, so to speak. Like other reptiles, snakes don't regulate their own body temperature internally. Instead they'll seek out warmer or cooler environments to adjust their temperatures. Snakes certainly don't want to cuddle up with you at night to stay warm though.

Additional facts: Another snake myth is that venomous snakes have vertical pupils while nonvenomous snakes have round pupils. This holds true for some species, but there are exceptions. Always enjoy snakes from a respectable distance, and you'll never have any troubles.

GROW YOUR OWN MOLD

Mold doesn't exactly have the greatest reputation. After all, eating moldy food is just gross, and having mold inside a house or building is not healthy for breathing. It can still be fascinating to study though. Here's how to grow your own so you can take a closer look.

Supplies: Shoebox, newspaper, spray bottle, bread, apple core, piece of cheese, banana peel

Time: 10 minutes setup time; 1 to 2 weeks to grow mold

Observe and learn: Predict which object you have that will grow mold first. Then study the different kinds of mold you find and how they're different. You could also go on a hike and look for mold growing out in the wild. See how it compares.

HOW-TO:

1. Mold likes damp, moist areas. So your job is to re-create this in a controlled environment. No, you shouldn't use the space under your bed or a section of your basement! Instead, find a shoebox.
2. Line the shoebox with newspaper or other recycled paper just to give it an extra barrier in case the insides get really damp.
3. Take a piece of bread and lightly spray it with water. Then place it inside the shoebox. Next place the box in a cool, dark spot. Check on your bread every couple of days, and if the bread seems like it is drying out, moisten it again with your spray bottle. Be sure to take pictures of the process along the way. It'll be fun to compare day 1 with day 12.
4. Experiment with other items to see which grow mold fastest. An apple core, banana peel, and cheese are all good options to try.

Not a plant or animal, mold, along with mushrooms, is actually part of the huge fungi kingdom.

35: Lightning doesn't strike the same place twice.

MYTH SCALE: 3

About the myth: Lightning strikes are pretty rare. So by default the likelihood of the same spot being struck *twice* by lightning must be nearly impossible.

The truth: Lightning can indeed strike the same place twice. In fact, it is pretty common. Tall trees, mountain peaks, and the tops of buildings are all commonly on the receiving end of lightning. Some buildings use lightning rods to ensure that lightning strikes the same place time and time again. When properly installed and grounded, lightning rods act as the path of least resistance for the release of the electrical energy of lightning. This helps protect the surrounding areas from damages associated with getting struck.

The takeaway: While lightning strikes are rare, it's always a good idea to seek shelter from a storm. Weathercasters are great at tracking active storm systems. When they issue storm watches and storm warnings, you'd best pay attention. Worldwide, lightning is responsible for around 2,000 human deaths each year.

Additional facts: At any given second, there are more than one hundred lightning strikes flashing around the world.

36: Snapping turtles can't let go after they bite.

MYTH SCALE: 3

About the myth: Snapping turtles have strong jaws and are quick to bite, but can they let go? Some people think they can't let go until they hear thunder.

The truth: Snapping turtles have reached near-mythical status. They are elusive creatures by nature and are most active at night. Spending much of their lives in water, they often prefer to sit and wait for their prey to pass by. They can be most visible in the spring when the females search out sites to dig nests. This journey might take them across busy roads, so snapping turtles can unfortunately become roadkill victims. Also, you should resist any temptation to pull a turtle by the tail, as this can damage the spine.

Some people claim that once a snapping turtle bites, it can't open its mouth again. But it would be awfully hard to eat if you could only bite one time. Another popular claim is that once a turtle bites, it won't let go until it thunders. This isn't true.

The takeaway: You certainly don't want to get bit by a snapping turtle, but claims of their jaw strength have been stretched over the years. The jaw strength for snapping turtles is impressive, and their ridged shells and pointed mouths make them look much more intimidating than many other turtles.

Additional facts: Alligator snapping turtles of the southeastern United States have an appendage they use as fishing bait. They dangle this "worm" out of their mouths and then snap up fish that come in close to investigate.

SUMMER

37: Birds have no sense of smell.
MYTH SCALE: 2

About the myth: Many animals have a reputation for having a great sense of smell, but birds aren't really one of those animals. A lot of animals need their sense of smell to help them eat, but birds don't need that. They can just use their sense of sight instead.

The truth: For years scientists have thought that birds can't smell. Some people even suggest that if you want to keep squirrels away from your bird feeder, you can put hot pepper on your birdseed because birds can't smell it anyway. Recent studies, though, have suggested that we might not know as much as we thought. Scientists now have evidence that shows many examples of birds being able to smell to locate food. They also think birds can use their sense of smell to select mates, find nesting spots, and find food in the wild.

The takeaway: Scientists are always learning and studying animals, so what was true a few years ago isn't necessarily true today. Sure, they thought birds couldn't really smell much, but it's not the case. They're still learning about a bird's sense of smell and how it varies from one species to another, but they *can* smell!

Additional facts: Turkey vultures definitely use their sense of smell to locate food. One of their primary sources of food is roadkill and other decaying carcasses, which smell pretty awful to most people. If they couldn't smell, they wouldn't be able to locate this food.

Stranger than Fiction

TORNADOS ARE MORE COMMON IN THE UNITED STATES THAN ANY OTHER COUNTRY.

The United States has on average 1,200 tornados per year. This is more than four times the number of twisters that hit Europe each year. Although they have been recorded in all fifty states, there is a reason the central United States is the region known as Tornado Alley. It is based on geography. Low-pressure areas can form east of the Rocky Mountains, then cool arctic air and warmer air from the south collide. This combination of conditions can trigger tornados. Tornados can form classic funnel clouds, or they can take on a massive wedge shape. Small tornados can have circular winds between 65 and 85 miles per hour, while stronger systems top out at over 200 miles per hour.

There have never been any tornados documented in Antarctica.

38: Raccoons wash their food before eating it.

MYTH SCALE: 2

About the myth: If you've ever seen a cartoon with a raccoon in it, then there's a good chance it shows the raccoon washing its food. This has been the belief for years that before eating their food, raccoons will go and wash it in some kind of water because they prefer to eat it when it's clean.

The truth: Raccoons have very small, almost humanlike hands, and they have been observed putting their food in water before they eat it. So this is probably where the myth got started, but it's not really washing. Scientists still aren't sure why some raccoons like to wet their food before they eat it. Maybe they just like it that way. But even then, they don't always wet their food. Raccoons will raid bird feeders and garbage cans for food at night, and they aren't washing that food prior to eating it.

The takeaway: It looks like a raccoon is washing its food, but this isn't the case. Even if you see a raccoon holding food at a stream or underwater, it's not "washing" it like we do or how we might think.

Additional facts: Raccoons really do eat almost anything. They will eat eggs, garbage, fish, mice, and lots of other things. They come out at night to feed, so keep an eye out in your backyard for the chance to see a raccoon.

39: Birds explode if they eat rice.

MYTH SCALE: 3

About the myth: At the end of a wedding, when the bride and groom leave, it's been a long-standing tradition to shower them with rice as they run out. It's a way of wishing them well. But then a lot of people stopped doing this because they heard rice goes into a bird's stomach, expands, and then they explode. No one wants to kill innocent birds!

The truth: Rice will not do harm to birds. This myth is completely false. Now, there are other reasons not to throw rice at wedding. It's kind of messy, and it could potentially make someone fall if they try to walk on it. A lot of people now throw birdseed, though, which is a great option as well.

The takeaway: You don't have to worry about avoiding rice because of the birds. Even if they wanted to eat it (and they probably don't), they'd be just fine.

Additional facts: While rice doesn't harm birds, there is something else that people can throw into the air that can. Balloons can kill both birds and marine animals because of the material they are made from—then the animals eat it, which is very harmful. Releasing any balloon in the air can actually do a lot of harm, so be careful.

40: A turtle on its back can't flip back over.

MYTH SCALE: 3

About the myth: Think about a turtle for a second. Its body has a big job in holding up its shell. So what happens when a gust of wind comes along and knocks that turtle right over on its back? It doesn't seem like it'll ever be able to flip back over, does it?

The truth: This theory has been tested, and while it might seem next to impossible, turtles can flip themselves back over. Much like a little baby is learning to flip itself over or crawl, a turtle does so a little bit at a time. It just takes a couple of good moves to get the right angle and the right motion to flip back. You can even find videos online to show how turtles can flip from their backs.

The takeaway: You should never turn a turtle over to perform this test for yourself because it's not very respectful to the animal, but you don't need to worry about turtles either. They have grown accustomed to hauling around those big shells, and they'll be just fine if something happens.

Additional facts: Turtles have a reputation for being slow, but is that really the case? The short answer is yes. Turtles are very slow, in part because they have a big shell to haul around and little legs that don't move very fast. If you see a turtle on the side or middle of the road, go ahead and move it so it doesn't get hit by a car.

Luck Legends

IF A BUTTERFLY LANDS ON YOUR SHOULDER, GOOD THINGS ARE GOING TO HAPPEN.

Whether this one is true or not, who wouldn't want a butterfly to land on their shoulder? If you've ever been in a butterfly house, they'll tell you that butterflies are more likely to land on people wearing bright colors. Give this a try, and don't forget to be very still!

RAISE YOUR OWN BUTTERFLY

One of the most fascinating life cycles you can watch up close and personal is that of a butterfly. It's amazing to see a little caterpillar grow bigger and bigger each day before it forms a chrysalis and turns into a butterfly. Now it's time to watch and study this transformation for yourself.

Supplies: Caterpillar, caterpillar food, plastic container
Time: 2 to 3 weeks
Observe and learn: Study even the tiniest of details as you watch your caterpillar grow. How long does it take for it to double its size? How long is it in the chrysalis stage? Watch each stage carefully to better understand how the whole process works.

How-To:

1. First you're going to need a caterpillar. The easy way to get a caterpillar is to order a kit online. Chances are it'll be a painted lady caterpillar and will come with its own food. If you're adventurous, set out to find a caterpillar on a plant instead. Then place your caterpillar in a large clear container where you can observe it. Make sure there are air holes in the container.
2. Now that you have a caterpillar, you need to make sure it gets plenty of food. If you have a kit, it'll come with food. Otherwise, you need to feed your caterpillar lots of leaves of whatever you found it on. Many caterpillars need specific plants to survive (called host plants). So if you found your caterpillar on a specific plant, it's probably the right food.

3. Watch and observe as your caterpillar forms a chrysalis. Don't be discouraged if you don't see it doing anything for a while. It needs time to make that transformation into a butterfly.
4. Once your butterfly emerges, let it go so it can fly away and continue the cycle.

The entire process of caterpillar to butterfly usually takes anywhere from two to three weeks.

41: Male animals are bigger than female animals.

MYTH SCALE: 2

About the myth: It's easy to think that males of most species are bigger than females. We live in a culture where men, on average, are taller than women. So it's easy to think of all males as the larger, bigger, more dominant ones, even in the animal world.

The truth: It's true that with mammals, the males are often bigger than the females because they usually have the job of offering protection. But that's definitely not the case with all animals. With most insects, the female is actually bigger than the male. This is the case for a lot of birds, especially raptors, too. This is because females have the job of carrying young, so they need bigger bodies for this.

The takeaway: You can't assume that males are actually bigger. Even for mammals, you might come across a female that is bigger than her mate. Challenge yourself by observing animals at the zoo or on a farm or even the smaller animals like insects in your backyard. See if you can figure out which one is male and which is female by using a good guidebook.

Additional facts: Here's a fun phrase to learn: sexual dimorphism. When sexual dimorphism exists in species, it means that males and females have distinct things that make them look different. When it doesn't exist, it means they look exactly the same and it's hard to tell the difference between them by appearance only.

Luck Legends

IF A BIRD COMES TOWARD YOU, YOU WILL HAVE BAD LUCK.

Many cultures have looked toward birds to give them signs of what's ahead. There are a lot of differing opinions about what it means when birds fly to you, away from you, horizontally, and so on. This one warns of birds flying toward you. Bad luck or not, it's a cool opportunity to get a closer look at the bird, so take it!

Stranger than Fiction

THERE ARE MORE UNKNOWN SPECIES IN THE OCEAN THAN KNOWN ONES.

Nearly 70 percent of the earth's surface is ocean, making our planet the Blue Planet. But how much do we know about what is going on below the surface of the ocean? Not as much as you might think. Currently there are about 226,000 known species living in the oceans. That sounds like a lot, right? But some researchers think there are two or three times as many species still left to describe. Most of these critters will be the smallest of creatures—things like phytoplankton, crustaceans, and mollusks. There are still larger species yet to be discovered too. Perhaps even some whales and dolphins. As you can imagine, the oceans can be difficult to study. But if you become a marine biologist, you might get to discover a new species.

New species are discovered on land every year too. Not just microscopic things either, even new birds and mammals are found.

42: Touching a toad will give you warts.

MYTH SCALE: 3

About the myth: It's been a long-standing belief that you shouldn't touch toads because they will give you warts. The myth says that you should avoid touching toads altogether, and if you do happen to come into contact with a toad, you should wash up thoroughly.

The truth: This myth probably got started in large part because toads have dry, bumpy skin, and it looks like they have warts all over their body. So people assumed that warts came from toads because they look the same. This is impossible though. Warts are actually a type of human virus, not something you get from other animals.

The takeaway: You absolutely cannot get a wart from a toad. So feel free to pick up that little toad you find hopping along in your backyard. Feel its skin and notice how rough and bumpy it is. Then, as with anything else, wash your hands when you're done. Not because you might get a wart but because it's just a good hygiene practice overall.

Additional facts: You know those bumps that look like warts on a toad's body? Those are equipped with something called parotid glands. These release a substance that can be harmful to predators. It's not going to hurt you in any way, but it's a pretty cool tool that helps them avoid being eaten!

43: If you get bitten by a snake, you can suck the venom out.

MYTH SCALE: 3

About the myth: Let's say you're hiking with a friend in the woods. You're walking along and a snake reaches out and bites you on the leg. You remember hearing that someone can suck out the venom from your leg, so you turn to your friend and hope he or she will agree.

The truth: There are many issues with this myth. First of all, not that many snakes are venomous. So even if a snake bites you, you don't know that it's going to do much harm, though it does hurt! Second of all, snakes aren't really prone to bite. If you step directly on them or threaten them, they might. But a snake isn't just going to come up and bite you for no reason. And finally, sucking out the venom could do more harm than good. You can't even be sure that it's going to work. And even if it does work, your friend could have the venom in his or her mouth, which isn't a good thing either. Even if your friend intends to spit it out, it's not a smart thing to do.

The takeaway: The best thing to do is to consult a medical doctor. The chance of a snake biting you in the wild is pretty slim, and most likely you'll be close enough to call someone or get attention so you can get medical help. This is an area where it's really best not to put matters into your hands.

Additional facts: Here's a fun little fact about snakes: Even though they have fangs, they don't chew their food like we do. They might use their fangs to bite their food, but then they don't chew up the pieces— they actually swallow most of their food whole.

Luck Legends

This is not an easy task to accomplish. While scientists don't know for sure, they estimate that there might be only one four-leaf clover for every 10,000 three-leaf clovers. It's a good challenge to take on. Find a nice sunny day and a big clover patch. Then start looking. Don't forget to take a picture with your treasure if you find one!

44: Spiders are insects.

MYTH SCALE: 3

About the myth: When you think of insects, what comes to mind? You probably think of something small with little legs that crawls around. With this in mind, it would be easy to assume that spiders are part of the insect family.

The truth: Spiders have a whole category of their own—arachnids. Mites, ticks and scorpions are some of the other crawly critters that are in this group. What are the differences between spiders and insects? Take a look. To begin with, spiders do not have antennae like insects do. They also have eight legs, compared to insects' six. Finally, insects have bodies made up of three parts, while spiders have bodies in two parts.

The takeaway: Spiders are really in a class all their own. The next time you are outside, see if you can find a spider and an insect and really try to notice the differences between the two. Don't forget to grab your magnifying glass.

Additional facts: Fear of spiders is called arachnophobia, and it affects a lot of people. Some studies say that as many as 50 percent of women are scared of spiders.

45: You can calculate temperature by counting cricket chirps.

MYTH SCALE: 2

About the myth: Here's how the myth goes: You count the number of times a cricket chirps in 14 seconds. Then you add 40, and you'll get the temperature in degrees Fahrenheit. If you want to get the degrees in Celsius, count the number of chirps in 25 seconds, divide by 3, and then add 4.

The truth: Can you really count on chirping crickets to help you determine the weather? This myth is highly debated because some people swear that it really works. They say the temperature won't be exact, but it will be within a few degrees. Other people say the equation is off, and there's just too much room for error to get an accurate read.

The takeaway: It is true that crickets chirp faster when the temperature heats up and slower when temperatures fall, but it's probably not the best way to calculate temperature. It's a good test to try out for yourself, but it's more for fun than anything else.

Additional facts: The cricket-chirping temperature method goes all the way back to 1897 and physicist A. E. Dolbear. He published the first equation for calculating temperature (which varies a little bit from the one above). It was called Dolbear's Law.

Stranger than Fiction

DRAGONS ARE REAL . . . SORT OF.

Dragon*flies* are real, that is! They don't breathe fire, but they are still awesome. Dragonflies have been around since the days of the dinosaurs. Back then they were much larger, some even had 2-foot wingspans. Talk about impressive! Today's dragonflies are still fierce predators. They are quick and agile insect eaters. Some species can cruise up to 35 miles per hour as they patrol the edges of ponds and meadows. Dragonflies also have crazy eyes with over 30,000 lenses. This lets them see all around them, but the trade-off is that they can't see details very well at all. Next time you are out on a hike, impress your friends by showing them a real dragon!

A myth about dragonflies is that they can bring dead snakes back to life. They are sometimes called snake doctors based on this false belief.

46: Shooting stars are stars falling out of the sky.

MYTH SCALE: 3

About the myth: You're out gazing at stars at night when you suddenly see a flash of light speed across the sky. You feel lucky to have witnessed this moment. Shooting stars are supposed to be pretty rare, and you're supposed to make a wish upon one when you see it. How cool that you just saw a star falling out of the sky!

The truth: Are you ready for it? You know those "stars" you see shooting across the sky? They're actually not stars at all! You can blame all those movies and cartoons you've seen that make shooting stars seem so rare and magical. What you're seeing up in the sky is actually a streak of light produced from a piece of a meteor. You often see just one at a time, but sometimes you can see several, which is known as a meteor shower.

The takeaway: Even though you now know shooting stars are actually meteors, it's still cool to see one. If you still want to make a wish on it, just for fun, go right ahead. Just tell your friends that you're wishing on a shooting meteor!

Additional facts: Watching a meteor shower is an amazing experience. It looks like dozens of "shooting stars" zooming across the sky. If you check out a local astronomy organization or find a calendar online of when meteor showers are supposed to happen in your area, you can plan for it. It's definitely an experience you have to see for yourself.

LIGHTNING BUGS GLOW THROUGH BIOLUMINESCENCE.

Lightning bugs, also known as fireflies, are incredible insects. Their trademark blinking lights are caused by a chemical reaction in the abdomen of the bug. "Bioluminescence" is the fancy term for this. Other things that have bioluminescence include single-celled bacteria and dinoflagellates, and even larger things like fish and squid.

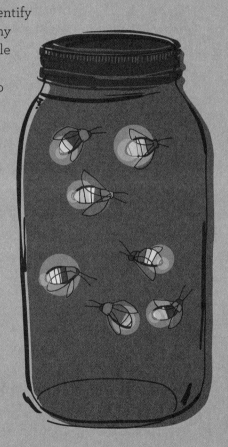

The frequency of flashing can help identify the 2,000 different species of fireflies. Many use their flashing to attract mates. A couple of species are predatory. They mimic the flashes of other species, tricking them into coming close enough to get eaten. None of this biology matters when you're running around the backyard trying to catch fireflies. What technique works best for you? Trying to grab one out of the air? Stalking one that is on the ground flashing? Perhaps sitting and waiting for a firefly to come to you? Go ahead and catch a couple of lightning bugs. Keep them in a jar and observe them closely for a short while, but be sure to release them back to where you caught them.

There are some species of lightning bugs that don't produce light at all.

47: If a plant is wilting, it needs water.

MYTH SCALE: 1

About the myth: When it comes to plants, everyone knows they need water. This is one of the most important things you can do to have success as a gardener. So if you see a plant looking a little weak or wilting, you should always add water.

The truth: Plants definitely need water, and they often do wilt a little bit if you forget to water them. So a wilting plant can sometimes be a good reminder to add water. But a wilting plant could be a sign of too much water too. If you are watering a plant every single day or multiple times a day, this is too much for it to handle. It can make the soil too moist, which leads to something called root rot.

The takeaway: Yes, there is such a thing as watering a plant too much. For a lot of plants, watering them every other day is enough. For others, it's best to water a little bit each day. Other factors come into play as well, like how dry or hot it is around the plant and how much rain you're getting. There really is no single way to water plants. As a good rule of thumb, you can feel the top of the soil for your plant. If it feels dry, it could use some water. If it feels damp, skip watering for a day or two.

Additional facts: Some people think you shouldn't water cacti at all because they're used to no water from living in the desert. This is not true! Cacti need water as well. Again, you don't want to overwater them, but if you get a cactus plant, make sure you read a little bit about it so you know how much to water.

Weather Legends

IF SOMEONE'S KNEE JOINT HURTS, THERE'S GOING TO BE RAIN.

Some people swear by this, saying they can predict the rain because their joints hurt. Often it's an older generation who uses this to predict the weather. Try doing a little survey of the people in your family to see if they notice any difference right before it rains.

48: You can tell how old a ladybug is by the number of its spots.

MYTH SCALE: 3

About the myth: This one makes a lot of sense, right? As a ladybug gets older, it gains more spots. So if you count them up, you can tell how old it is.

The truth: The number of spots a ladybug has actually has nothing to do with its age. Spots do matter, though. There's more than just one kind of ladybug out there, and the pattern of spots can tell you what kind it is.

The takeaway: It's a lot of fun to count a ladybug's spots, so count away! But the number isn't actually a way to predict its age.

Additional facts: The red and black color combination is one that many insect-eating animals have learned to leave alone. The colors are like a big warning sign to say STAY AWAY!

49: Eating carrots will improve your eyesight.

MYTH SCALE: 2

About the myth: It seems like the perfect solution! Maybe you have glasses you wear that you'd like to get rid of. Or perhaps you just want to have superhero eyesight so you can see objects from a mile or more away. What's the answer? Eat carrots! Wouldn't it be great if those orange veggies were the solution?

The truth: Here's the thing—carrots have beta-carotene. Your body coverts this to vitamin A, which is also important for overall good eye health. In fact, an extreme lack of vitamin A can actually lead to blindness. So yes, in some ways, carrots contribute to good health (and good eye health) overall. But this does not mean that if you eat carrots, you'll be able to see better or avoid needing eyeglasses. Should you still eat your carrots? Yep! They are sweet and tasty and a healthy food.

The takeaway: There's a reason your mom, grandma, teacher, and other adults have been telling you to eat your veggies. They are good for you! If you can learn to love veggies now, you'll start a healthy habit that will serve you well for years. Veggies have essential nutrients and natural health benefits, and garden-fresh ones are even better for taste and nutrition! Consider growing your own or hitting your local farmers' market.

Additional facts: Want to know some other foods that have good beta-carotene in them? Nearly all orange fruits and veggies are a good source—mangos, pumpkins, sweet potatoes, apricots, and butternut squash. For another source, try almost any type of leafy green like lettuce, kale, or spinach. Here's one more fun fact—if you eat too many carrots, the beta-carotene can make your skin look yellowish!

Be a Scientist

MAKE SUN PRINTS

The sun is a pretty powerful thing—no wonder sunscreen is so important to wear! Just see how powerful those rays can be and use them to your advantage with this little experiment. You'll be creating some fun art at the same time!

Supplies: Sun paper, objects to make prints
Time: 5 minutes to prep; a few hours to make prints
Observe and learn: Practice with different shapes to see which ones make the best prints. See if it's better to use large objects or smaller ones. Also try making a sun print in a couple of hours and making one after 6+ hours in the sun.

How-To:

1. For best results on this project, you're going to want to invest in some special sun paper. Just do a search online for sun print paper or sun art, and you'll soon have lots of options to choose from. You can also check out your local arts-and-crafts store to see if they carry sun paper.
2. Use this project as an excuse to go out and find objects in nature from which you want to make a print. Leaves are very popular for making sun prints. Gather up single leaves or a branch from a flower. You can also try household objects like cookie cutters or other shapes.
3. Read the instructions that come with your sun paper, but you should be able to just place your objects on the paper (make sure they are secure) and then put them out in the sun.
4. After a few hours, you'll have prints on your paper. Frame your new artwork and hang it up.

It will take longer, but try making a sun print on a dishcloth as well. Tape on leaves and then leave it in the sun for several weeks.

50: If you swallow a watermelon seed, you'll grow one in your stomach.

MYTH SCALE: 3

About the myth: Most watermelons are filled with seeds (unless you buy or grow a seedless variety). It's just part of eating and enjoying a watermelon—you have to spit out the seeds. Watch out though. Those slippery little things are easy to swallow, and if the old saying holds true, you could be growing a watermelon in your stomach!

The truth: Have you ever heard of the term "tall tale"? It's something that is so silly and ridiculous that it could pretty much never come true. Yet it's often passed on from one generation to the next as being true. At least, they want you to think it's true. This is one of those tall tales. For years, adults have been telling kids that they shouldn't swallow watermelon seeds because something could start growing in their stomachs. This is not true at all—not even a little bit! Watermelon seeds, or any seeds for that matter, cannot sprout in your stomach.

The takeaway: You should enjoy your watermelon and not be afraid of eating it. Most people still spit the seeds out, but if you accidently swallow one on occasion, it's not the end of the world. In fact, a lot of people even like roasting watermelon seeds just like you would pumpkin seeds.

Additional facts: Watermelons are pretty heavy, right? Well a whopping 92 percent of that weight is actually water. You can probably tell too. When you bite into a watermelon, the juices run everywhere. Try making up some watermelon juice ice cubes to put in water. It's a fun little project to do, and they're delicious.

51: Mushroom fairy rings are rare.

MYTH SCALE: 2

About the myth: If you're hiking in the meadow or forest and come across a distinct circle of mushrooms, it's a pretty eye-catching sight. It's easy to think this is a rare occurrence. You might even remember that some people say you should make a wish in a fairy ring and then it will come true.

The truth: Fairy rings definitely look cool. They seem to come out of nowhere, and they do almost seem magical because you wonder how all those mushrooms got to grow in such a well-formed circle. They aren't all that rare though. While it's most common for them to occur in or around forests, you can see them in backyards as well. Whether they are lucky or not is a whole new question, but it never hurts to make a wish.

The takeaway: While fairy rings aren't rare, they might be rare to you. If you come across one, enjoy it. Step into the middle to make a wish and take a few pictures too. Take time to admire the ring and the mushrooms growing. Are they all the same size and shape? What does the grass or ground look like underneath the ring? Even when the mushrooms die, you can often still see the shadow of a ring on the grass. Keep an eye out for that as well.

Additional facts: How do you tell poisonous mushrooms from ones you can eat? If you don't know, it's probably best to just leave it. Otherwise, use a mushroom book. You can check one out at your local library. This will give you a better idea of what is poisonous and what isn't.

Stranger than Fiction

SNAKES SMELL WITH THEIR TONGUES.

Why are snakes always sticking out their tongues? To smell! You'd stick your tongue out too if it functioned as your nose. Snakes do have nostrils, but the tongue plays an essential role in sniffing out prey and detecting pheromones (chemical signals). You see, snakes have a highly developed part of their body called the vomeronasal organ. The snakes use their tongues to flick sensory information through this organ. The coolest part is that the forked tongue of the snake allows it to detect from which direction the smells are coming. It is kind of like three-dimensional smelling.

Another name for the vomeronasal organ is Jacobson's organ, for the researcher who discovered it. Other animals have Jacobson's organs as well, but none are as specialized as the snake's.

52: If a jellyfish stings you, have someone pee on the injured spot.

MYTH SCALE: 3

About the myth: TV shows, movies, and even books have encouraged this myth. Here's how the story goes—someone is swimming in the ocean when a jellyfish stings them. They are in so much pain that they beg someone to pee on the sting to help make the pain go away.

The truth: While this makes a funny story, it's not actually true. When a jellyfish stings you, the area will be angry, red, and painful. It's tempting to do anything to ease the pain, but it honestly won't do any good.

The takeaway: If a jellyfish does sting you, it's best to rinse the area thoroughly with salt water. If you need medical attention, seek a doctor and not your friend!

Additional facts: The stinging cells in jellyfish tentacles do serve a purpose. They are used to help the jellyfish capture food.

53: All bugs are bad for the garden.

MYTH SCALE: 2

About the myth: It can take a lot of work to make a garden look beautiful, so if you go outside to find a bunch of bugs destroying your plants or eating your veggies, you want them gone. You might do anything to get rid of them so you can have a bug-free backyard.

The truth: Before you grab that bug-killing spray, you should really look at the bugs you're getting in your backyard. Most bugs you find in the garden aren't actually bad bugs at all. In fact, many of the good bugs will actually get rid of the bad bugs without you having to do a thing. If you just spray something, there's a good chance you're going to kill *all* the bugs in your backyard, including good spiders, caterpillars, and more. Think about that for a second. If you kill all the caterpillars in your backyard, you're not going to have butterflies either. And what about bees? Flowers need bees to pollinate flowers, so you don't want to go and kill them.

The takeaway: All good gardens have bugs. Yes, there are some bad bugs out there that you can control on a case-by-case basis, but don't try to get rid of all the bugs. You need them to have healthy plants. Before you go eliminating bugs, do a little bit of additional research to see if you can figure out what you have.

Additional facts: Beetles are one of those bugs that often get a bad reputation. In some cases, as with Japanese beetles, they can take over backyards and kill plants. But in many other cases, beetles are part of a healthy backyard. For instance, ladybugs are beetles, and they are a good bug to have because they will help get rid of bad bugs.

Stranger than Fiction

SOME CICADAS STAY UNDERGROUND FOR SEVENTEEN YEARS.

Most bugs have short life spans, and this holds true for many cicadas too. But there are a few species of cicada that have incredibly long lives. You might be old enough to vote before you get a chance to see these species. Periodical cicadas can live underground for seventeen years! Others spend thirteen years underground. The nymphs of cicadas live underground. They can be up to a foot below the surface, feeding on plant roots. Adult cicadas only come aboveground for a short period, say four to six weeks in the summer.

Around an inch long, adult cicadas are hefty insects. They have thick bodies, big eyes, and long, clear wings. They are pretty gnarly to look at but are harmless. They do make quite a ruckus of noise as they try to attract mates. After mating, the females lay eggs, all the adults die off, and the cicadas aren't seen for another seventeen years.

You don't necessarily have to wait seventeen years to see a cicada. Different species of periodical cicada are on different seventeen-year cycles. There are also annual cicada species that are out every summer.

54: Poison ivy is contagious.

MYTH SCALE: 3

About the myth: Have you heard the phrase "Leaves of three, let it be"? This is because poison ivy has three leaves, and it's an easy way to remember what to stay away from. Then if you get the poison ivy rash, be careful! You don't want it to spread.

The truth: When you come into contact with poison ivy, it has an oil on it that makes some people react and develop a rash. But the oil doesn't stay with the rash. If you have a poison ivy rash and then someone brushes up against it, they are not going to suddenly be affected by poison ivy. Also, it can take several days or even a couple of weeks for a rash to form. If two people come into contact with poison ivy at the same time, one person might develop a reaction immediately, while the other one might develop a reaction a week or two later. This is because reactions differ from one person to the next. Someone with poison ivy can't "give" it to another person.

The takeaway: You should avoid poison ivy growing in the wild because it can cause an itchy, annoying, and even painful rash. You don't have to worry about the rash being contagious though. If you do come into contact with poison ivy, it's best to thoroughly wash your skin to remove any oils and also wash your clothes. The oil can stay on clothes and be contagious that way.

Additional facts: Poison ivy doesn't affect everyone. Studies show that about 85 percent of people are allergic to poison ivy. This is a pretty big majority, so you probably shouldn't risk it. But this might explain why some people don't seem to be affected by poison ivy at all.

Be a Scientist

CREATE HOMES FOR BACKYARD ANIMALS

Supplies: Sticks, flowerpot, old bricks, dirt, wood (depending on the type of animal)

Time: 20 minutes

Observe and learn: Talk about what makes a good home for an animal. All animals want to feel safe and secure, right? Think about this and how you can help as you're creating homes for animals in your backyard.

How-To:

1. Before you start creating animal homes, you need to do a little research. What types of homes do animals use? Go on a hike and do a little research to figure out what types of animals you can create homes for.

2. For this project, let's build a home for a toad and the bugs in your backyard. You want these animals to feel safe, so you want to offer them lots of cover. For the toad, you can turn a flowerpot on its side to immediately create a little haven. For bugs, you'll want to stack up sticks, bricks, wood, and other items to give them little places to crawl.

3. After you create the homes, you need to leave them alone! Animals don't like it if you go in and mess around in places they live. It won't feel safe to them. So you can observe, but don't move things around too much.

4. If you don't see any animals moving in right away, don't give up. You can try building something in a different location to see if it makes a difference. For the best results, you'll want to put something out of the open—tucked away in a cool, slightly dark location.

Of course, you can always create an animal home by putting out a birdhouse too. But did you know that most birds don't even use birdhouses? Look for nesting birds on tree branches and in tree cavities.

Weather Legends

IF COWS ARE LYING DOWN, YOU WILL HAVE BAD WEATHER.

Look at that cow over there! Is it just tired or is it giving us a warning sign that rain is on the way? Yes, cows do lie down when they get tired. They don't just stand around all the time. But this myth (sometimes it's told about horses too) has been passed around for years.

55: You shouldn't swim for at least 30 minutes after you eat.

MYTH SCALE: 3

About the myth: Some sources say you should wait for 30 minutes. Others say 45 minutes or even an hour. No matter what the exact number, it's said to be safer this way. Then your blood can go to your digestive system to help digest food. Otherwise, you won't have good blood flow in your arms and legs as you're trying to swim.

The truth: This myth is completely false. There's really no truth in it at all. Perhaps a bunch of parents made it up because they wanted to take a break after lunch instead of watching their kids swim? This myth has been passed on for generations, but it's really not dangerous or harmful to swim right after you eat.

The takeaway: Now you don't have to worry about taking a break from swimming to eat. You can keep swimming right after you have your snack or meal. If you're swimming, it's better to practice other safe habits like wearing sunscreen or a life vest while going in deep waters.

Additional facts: Have you ever seen a dog swim? Take a look and you'll see where the term "dog paddle" came from. Dogs swim with their heads sticking out of the water as they quickly paddle their feet. To do this yourself, just keep your head out of the water and stay afloat kicking your feet and using your arms to tread water.

56: Sharks kill a lot of people.

MYTH SCALE: 3

About the myth: As you're splashing in the ocean, you see the hint of a shark fin in the distance. It starts to circle someone out in the water. If you believe what you see in the movies, this person is about to get attacked and could be this shark's next meal.

The truth: Most sharks do not attack. In fact, they don't even come near shore where they would come in contact with humans. Out of all the shark species out there (there are more than 300), only a very small handful will even attack a person. And even in those few instances, it's usually because they are confused, not because they are out to eat them. (Humans are not really part of a shark's diet.) There are many other animals that are considered more deadly to humans than sharks, including horses, cows, ants, deer, bees, and hippopotamuses.

The takeaway: We actually do more harm to sharks than they do to us. By fishing the ocean, it's taking away their food supply. The next time you have a chance to see a shark (probably in an aquarium of some sort), take a closer look at it, and try to gain a new appreciation for sharks. They are pretty cool animals. They just get a bad reputation because of a few movies out there!

Additional facts: Sharks have a lot of teeth! They lose them a lot too, but they can quickly grow replacements. Some studies show that sharks can have as many as 30,000 teeth during their lifetimes.

57: When planting you should dig a hole twice the width and depth of the plant.

MYTH SCALE: 2

About the myth: Plants can be sensitive when you first plant them. You want to do everything in your power to make sure you have a successful garden, so it makes sense to give them plenty of space. Some people suggest the hole should be twice the width and depth of the whole plant, while others say it's just twice the size of the root ball. (The root ball is what comes out of the planter that goes into the ground.)

The truth: Some plants are really big! Some root balls are really big! So just think about that for a second—what if you dug a hole that was really twice that size? Your plant would likely sink into the ground and the dirt would pile up along the sides. Yes, you're probably safe to dig out a width twice the size. This is a good idea because it gives your plant plenty of space to spread out from the very beginning. Just make sure you don't dig up surrounding plants that might be growing.

The takeaway: It's important to be careful when it comes to how deep you bury a plant. If you don't dig a hole deep enough, the roots will be exposed. If it's too deep, you could cover up too much of the plant. Use your best judgment. The soil should come up to about the same height of where the plant was in the planter.

Additional facts: Want another way to ensure you'll be a successful gardener? Water! Water is especially important when you first plant something. Some people even like to plant on a wet or rainy day so there's already a bit of moisture in the ground. After you finish planting a new plant, make sure to water it thoroughly the same day and the next day too.

Stranger than Fiction

MOUNTAINS AND VOLCANOES ARE IN THE OCEAN.

When you think about mountains and volcanoes, you picture them towering above the landscape, right? The peaks are even measured in elevation above sea level. In North America, at 20,320 feet, Denali is the highest mountain, while the highest volcano is Pico de Orizaba at 18,491 feet. But what if we look below the ocean? The midocean range stretches throughout the oceans, and it's by far the longest stretch of mountains on Earth. Most of the world's volcanic activity is associated with the midocean range too. You can find mountains and volcanoes completely under the sea. A few of the giant peaks stick out above the water, creating islands. The islands of Hawaii, for example, are mostly underwater mountain and volcano peaks. Mauna Kea, a volcano in Hawaii, is an impressive 13,800 feet above sea level. If you measure from the ocean floor though, it measures a whopping 33,500 feet tall. That's taller than Mount Everest.

Although they aren't underwater, the Appalachian Mountains are some of the oldest mountains in North America, while the Teton Mountains comprise one of the youngest ranges.

58: Skunk spray is pee.

MYTH SCALE: 3

About the myth: It isn't smart to mess with a skunk—you could get peed on. And the smell of skunk pee is the worst. And once it gets into your clothes or on your dog's hair, it is nearly impossible to remove.

The truth: Skunks eat just about anything, and they can show up in even the most urban of settings. Make no mistake: You want to give skunks plenty of space whenever you see one. If threatened, skunks will hiss and stomp their feet. They might even lift their tail up as a warning sign. As a last resort skunks will fire off a cloud of spray in self-defense. It isn't pee though. It is a separate spray made up of irritating and stinky chemical compounds.

The takeaway: Skunk spray is a unique compound that is squirted out of specialized glands. It isn't pee, but that doesn't make it any more appealing if you get some on you.

Additional facts: So how do you get rid of skunk smell? It is a myth that tomato paste or juice is the trick. Hydrogen peroxide is your best bet. It is most effective at neutralizing those stinky thiol chemicals that cause that rotten smell.

59: All weeds are bad.

MYTH SCALE: 3

About the myth: Ugh, weeds. They are annoying. They get in the tiniest of places. They take water away from the plants in your garden. And they're pretty ugly. Weeding is no fun either. Wouldn't it be easier if all weeds just went away?

The truth: Now this might come as a surprise to you, but there are lots of weeds out there that are good weeds! Yep. A lot of people think of milkweed as a weed because they see it growing along the side of the road, but it serves a very important role for monarch butterflies. And a lot of people hate dandelions growing in their yards, but they can provide birds with lots of food too!

The takeaway: Just because a plant has traditionally been known as a weed or has *weed* in the name doesn't mean it's bad. This doesn't mean you should love all weeds though. There are lots of weedy and invasive plants you should avoid. "Invasive" means it can take over in your backyard and threaten some of your native plants—this is not a good thing. And the tricky thing about these is that they can often look like pretty flowers that you want to plant. Honeysuckle is a good example. Some types of honeysuckle are really bad and can choke out other plants. The best thing to do is try to figure out what you have, and then make a call.

Additional facts: You can often find out about the weedy or invasive plants in your area by doing a quick online search. Just type in your area or state along with "invasive plant" or "weeds." This can help you get a start in figuring out what something is. For a national source, look at plants.usda.gov.

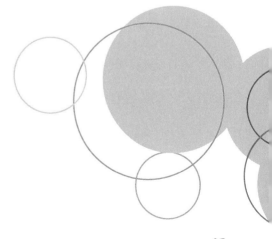

60: Rabbits love carrots.

MYTH SCALE: 2

About the myth: "What's up, Doc?" asks a certain cartoon rabbit. If carrots are Bugs Bunny's favorite snacks, aren't they the favorite food for the cottontails running around your neighborhood as well?

The truth: Bunnies will nibble on carrots, but they can't live on carrots alone. In the wild, rabbits tend to eat vegetation. This can include veggies but consists of mostly grasses and herbs. Rabbit teeth grow throughout the animal's entire life, but they are worn down by all of the chewing that rabbits do. Rabbits have two sets of upper front teeth. The second pair is directly behind the front pair. These small teeth are sometimes referred to as peg teeth. The peg teeth are one way scientists determined that rabbits weren't closely related to rodents like mice and rats.

The takeaway: Both celery and broccoli growers tried to convince the creators of Bugs Bunny to switch to these vegetables, but thanks to that cartoon, rabbits will always be associated with carrots. Even though rabbits would rather eat the leafy green tops than the orange carrots.

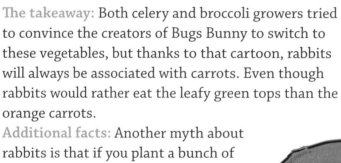

Additional facts: Another myth about rabbits is that if you plant a bunch of marigolds around your vegetable garden, it'll keep the bunnies out.

Stranger than Fiction

SOME PLANTS EAT MEAT.

While it isn't quite the same as animal predators eating meat, certain species of plants are carnivorous. The most famous of all is the Venus flytrap. Venus flytraps are found in the wild wetlands of the Carolinas. The plants get nutrients from the soil and air, but eating insects adds a nice boost of nutrients. The insect "traps" are modified leaves. When an insect lands and moves, the leaf closes up. If the insect is too small, it can escape the grip of the plant. Otherwise, the leaves close tightly around the unfortunate bug. It then takes about ten days for the plant enzymes to fully digest the insect.

Many greenhouses grow Venus flytraps, so you can have a pet plant. You'll still have to remember to feed and water it just like you would a dog or a cat though.

61: Lobsters are red.

MYTH SCALE: 2

About the myth: Lobsters are a tasty treat for many people. They are a classic menu item in Maine. In addition to being found on dinner plates, they are also featured on some Maine license plates. The red crustacean is an icon for the state.

The truth: In the wild, lobsters come in a lot of different colors. They can be brownish to olive green. Some might have hints of red that you can see, but they certainly aren't bright red. They only turn that way after being heated up—like in a pot of boiling water. The red pigments in lobsters are stable in heat, so while the other colors fade away, the red intensifies. It can take a lobster many years before it grows large enough to be harvested. They can live to be over 100 years old and over 3 feet long. As they grow bigger and bigger, they molt out of their shells. This happens about once a year. It takes a while for the new shell to harden up. They spend most of their lives near the ocean floor, and during their soft phase, they try to hide under rocks even more than normal.

The takeaway: Lobsters are red, but only after they've been cooked. They are usually brownish or green when they are alive.

Additional facts: Not all lobsters have claws. The clawed lobsters, including the American lobster in Maine, are generally found in colder waters. Spiny lobsters (also called rock lobsters) tend to be found in warmer waters.

62: Mouthwash will keep mosquitoes away.

MYTH SCALE: 3

About the myth: Nearly everyone has a home remedy to keep the mosquitoes away. Some folks are convinced it takes a 100 percent DEET solution applied to your clothes. Others prefer solutions that are less chemical. Diets high in garlic are one example. Oftentimes repellents involve smearing strong-smelling things on your body, even mouthwash. But do they work?

The truth: Mosquitoes are attracted to carbon dioxide and heat. If you are alive, you are breathing out carbon dioxide and giving off heat. There is a bit of evidence that suggests mosquitoes will target some people over others, but this isn't entirely understood. This does help explain how some remedies might appear to work occasionally. You can try out a few of your own mosquito repellents. What works best for you?

The takeaway: Nothing is 100 percent effective at keeping mosquitoes away. What works for one person might not work for another. It might just be that that person doesn't get bitten by as many mosquitoes.

Additional facts: If you spend much time outside, it is safe to say you'll have mosquito bites at some point. There are almost as many home remedies for treating mosquito bites as there are for trying to keep mosquitoes from biting in the first place. Your best bet is an anti-itch cream.

Weather Legends

IF YOU HAVE A RED SKY IN THE MORNING, THE DAY'S WEATHER IS GOING TO BE BAD.

Here's how the rhyme goes: "Red sky at morning, sailors take warning . . . red sky at night, sailor's delight." They say this little phrase dates back more than 2,000 years. It was supposed to be a simple way for people at sea to predict the weather.

Stranger than Fiction

SOME ANIMALS CAN LIVE WITHOUT WATER.

Water is essential for human survival. It helps carry nutrients to our cells, flush out waste products, and cushion our joints. We can't even digest food properly without it. People can survive a couple of days without water, but after that, conditions are pretty desperate. So that makes it even more shocking that a few animals can survive without ever taking a sip of water. As you might guess, they live in areas that don't have much water to begin with, mainly deserts.

The champions of a waterless life are the kangaroo rats. They have specialized adaptations that help retain water that would normally be lost with most animals. Most impressively, their bodies can harness water from the seeds they eat. Kangaroo rats don't even drink water when it is available to them.

Kangaroo rats are named for kangaroos. Hopping along on their oversize hind feet, some are able to jump 7 or 8 feet in a single bound. Pretty impressive for a mouse!

63: Pelicans live by the ocean.

MYTH SCALE: 2

About the myth: Pelicans are the ultimate beach bums. They chill on the coast, feeding on fish, living their lives near the ocean.

The truth: There are two different species of pelicans that live in the United States. The brown pelican is common along the California coast as well as in the Gulf of Mexico and up the Atlantic as far north as the Chesapeake Bay. The American white pelican spends the winter in these coastal waters as well. But during the summer breeding season, American white pelicans move north. They nest on large bodies of water in the central and western United States and Canada. One of the largest colonies of American white pelicans nests on Yellowstone Lake in Yellowstone National Park. That's about as far from an ocean as you can get. There are eight different species of pelicans in the world, and they all generally nest in large colonies. The four brownish species usually nest in trees, and the four species of whitish pelicans prefer to nest on the ground.

The takeaway: All pelicans are fish eaters that live near water. Brown pelicans live by the ocean, but American white pelicans nest along waters far inland.

Additional facts: Pelicans have different fishing styles. American white pelicans swim together to round fish up for eating, while brown pelicans plunge-dive out of the air to catch a meal.

Weather Legends

IF YOU SEE GULLS PERCHED OR SITTING, BAD WEATHER IS COMING.
This weather myth is much like the cow one, using an animal resting to predict the weather. It's another case where sometimes gulls just have to rest, but then again, the legend probably gets it right every now and then.

64: Damselflies are female dragonflies.

MYTH SCALE: 3

About the myth: Males and females of the same species can look similar but slightly different. Damselflies and dragonflies look almost the same. *Damsel* is a term for females, even when they aren't in distress. That makes damselflies girls. By default that makes dragonflies males.

The truth: As logical as all of that sounds, it couldn't be further from the truth. First off, damselflies and dragonflies aren't the same species. There are actually loads of different species of each, and each of these species has males and females. Even though they look similar, there are a few different ways to tell damselflies and dragonflies apart. You can start by looking them in the eyes. Damselflies have eyes along the sides of the head, and these eyes are separated by a little bit of space. The eyes of dragonflies nearly touch each other and are closer to the top of the head. Another way to tell them apart is how they hold their wings. Damselflies hold their wings along their bodies, while dragonflies keep their wings held open.

The takeaway: Damselflies and dragonflies do have many things in common, including big eyes, long, skinny bodies, and those cool wings. They aren't the same species though. And all of the different species of damselflies and dragonflies have both males and females.

Additional facts: In total there are about 5,000 species of damselflies and dragonflies. Together they make up the order called Odonata, which means "toothed ones." Here's the thing though: They don't have teeth.

65: Peanuts grow on trees.

MYTH SCALE: 3

About the myth: Peanuts are nuts. It says so right in the name. Pea*nut*. They certainly aren't peas. Nuts grow on trees. So peanuts obviously grow on trees.

The truth: The thing about it is peanuts aren't nuts. Lots of "nuts" we like to eat aren't true nuts. Almonds aren't. Neither are cashews, pistachios, or pine nuts. Things like walnuts, chestnuts, and acorns are all examples of the true nuts. Nuts are like modified fruits. They have a seed on the inside of a hard shell instead of inside the more familiar soft, pulpy fruits. A peanut "shell" is more of a pod. Peanuts are members of the nitrogen-fixing legume family. You know what else are legumes? Beans, lentils, and peas! Peanut bushes grow a foot or two tall. They are unique plants because after the bush flowers, it sends runner shoots (called pegs) back underground. The peanut then fully develops underground. To harvest peanuts, the bush is dug up and left out for the peanuts to dry. Each peanut plant can produce between 25 and 50 peanuts.

The takeaway: Peanuts are great snacks. They aren't nuts though. And they don't grow on trees. They grow underground.

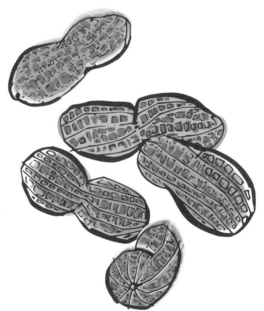

Additional facts: George Washington Carver is often credited for inventing peanut butter, but this isn't true. He did create hundreds of other uses for peanuts, and he also encouraged farmers to grow peanuts as a way to maintain soil quality.

Luck Legends

Here's how the rhyme goes: "Star light, star bright. First star I see tonight. I wish I may, I wish I might. Have this wish I wish tonight." If you whisper this little saying on the first star you see and then don't tell anyone your wish, it's supposed to come true.

66: Moths are always nocturnal.

MYTH SCALE: 1

About the myth: Moths are creatures of the night. You can see them swarming around your porch light after the sun goes down. When morning rolls around, they hunker down for the day.

The truth: Most moths are nocturnal, or active at night, but there are some exceptions. Some of the most spectacular moths are active during the day. This is called diurnal. Perhaps you've seen one but thought it was a butterfly. Or maybe you saw one of the sphinx moths flying around and you didn't even realize it. They hover around flowers, acting like a hummingbird. If you aren't paying attention, you might miss out on a cool moth sighting. Sure you'll see far more butterflies than moths during the daytime. The easiest way to tell moths apart from butterflies is to look at their antennae. Butterfly antennae have a little nob or club at the end. Moth antennae don't. Some moth antennae look almost like little feathers sprouting off their heads. Another thing to look for is that moths tend to hold their wings flat against the body, while butterflies hold their wings out vertically when resting.

The takeaway: You'll see the most moths after dark, but don't forget to look for moths during the day too.

Additional facts: Moths and butterflies are closely related. They are both classified as Lepidoptera. Moths make up around 90 percent of this group, while butterflies and skippers are just 10 percent.

67: June bugs are only visible in June.

MYTH SCALE: 2

About the myth: June bugs are so predictable, that's why they're called June bugs. As regularly as the sun rises every single morning, June bugs are out every June.

The truth: The eggs of June bugs are laid in the ground. The larvae hatch out and survive underground for a couple of years nibbling on grass roots and other plant matter. Adult June bugs tend to emerge in early summer. Around June in many parts of the United States it turns out. And while most adult June bugs are visible in June, that isn't always the case. Some can show up in May. Many folks call them May bugs in that case. Some come out in July, but for some reason nobody ever calls them July bugs. Whatever you call these bugs, they aren't true bugs at all. Instead they are beetles. There are hundreds of species, but they tend to be fairly drab and brownish. They also tend to be slow, clumsy fliers. It is like their bodies are too big for their wings. The beetles

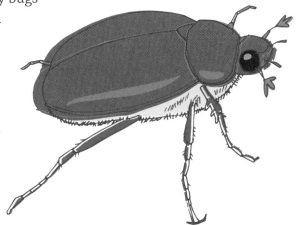

have elytra, which are modified wings. These create a firm protective layer on the back, but they don't help much with flight.

The takeaway: June bugs are most visible in June. Unless they are May bugs. Or June bugs that linger on into July. But they are still called June bugs.

Additional facts: Certain species of flies in the Pyrgotidae family can be parasites on June bugs. The flies lay their eggs on the backs of the beetles, underneath the elytra. When the eggs hatch they make a meal of the June bug.

Be a Scientist

MAKE A MINI-COMPOST BIN WITH WORMS

It's pretty cool when you can turn apple cores, banana peels, eggshells, and coffee grounds into soil through composting. It's not just regular soil either. It's gorgeous, rich, dark soil that is perfect for growing plants. Now add worms into the mix—they make the process even faster—and it's even more fun!

Supplies: Recycled ice-cream bucket, soil, newspaper, red wiggler worms
Time: 20 minutes
Observe and learn: Don't overdo it. Your worms are pretty amazing, but they aren't miracle workers. Start off small and see what they can handle. Watch them closely and increase what you give them a little at a time.

How-To:

1. An old ice-cream bucket makes the perfect vessel for a mini-composting bin. You'll want to make sure to add holes to the top of it, but don't make those holes too big. Red wiggler worms are small and could easily escape!
2. Fill your ice-cream bucket with about 50 percent soil and 50 percent "brown" matter like shredded newspaper or even little pieces of cardboard. You don't want the bucket to get too damp.
3. Add your worms to the mixture and give them a couple of days to make themselves at home. It's really important that you use red wiggler worms, not just worms you dig up in your backyard. Not all worms can eat and digest scraps.
4. Add a few kitchen scraps to your mixture and give your worms time to eat the items. As they eat it, they will turn the scraps into soil and mix it in with the other soil and newspaper.

5. If you're successful on a small level, move your worm compost into a bigger container and add more worms.

Worm composting is called vermicomposting. It's where you use worms to speed up the process of composting. The worms eat the scraps and poop it out to make great garden soil.

ice cream

68: A snake in the water can't bite.

MYTH SCALE: 3

About the myth: Even if you love snakes, you sure don't want to get bitten by one. Have you ever heard that a snake in the water can't bite? The story goes one of two ways: Either a snake can't bite when it is underwater or a snake can't bite while swimming on the water because it can't coil up and strike.

The truth: There are numerous species of snakes that are excellent swimmers—not just water snakes and water moccasins (cotton-mouths). Many snakes will eat frogs and minnows. It'd be hard to eat a minnow if you couldn't bite underwater! Snakes can't lunge very far on land, and even less so on water, but that doesn't mean they can't bite if something or someone gets too close. Lots of times snakes will be sunning themselves along the edge of the water, perhaps on a rock or a log. If they sense something approaching, they'll often get in the water and swim to safety. You might not even know they were ever there.

The takeaway: Snakes in the water, just like snakes on the land, tend to retreat from people if they have that option, so you should be cautious but not scared. If they feel cornered and are harassed, they will bite in self-defense.

Additional facts: In 1999 the Lake Erie water snake was protected as a threatened species under the Endangered Species Act. Through conservation and education efforts, the species was removed from the list by 2011.

69: Snakes and lizards are slimy.

MYTH SCALE: 3

About the myth: If you've never touched a snake or a lizard, how do you think it would feel? They don't have any hair, so they must be cold and slimy, right? They sure aren't warm and fuzzy like mammals.

The truth: Snakes and lizards aren't slimy at all. None of the reptiles are. They are all covered in scales. Sometimes these scales can be quite small and smooth. This can give them a shiny appearance, so it is understandable that people would think snakes and lizards would be slimy. But they aren't. Amphibians like frogs and salamanders can have a bit of mucus on the skin that gives them a slimy feel. Amphibians lack scales, so they use mucus to keep themselves from drying out too much. But not all amphibians are slimy either. Toads have pretty dry skin, kind of like snakes and lizards.

The takeaway: Snakes and lizards are reptiles. They are covered in scales, but they aren't slimy. Remember a few snakes and lizards could potentially be dangerous, so use caution. Also, if you do handle one for a quick inspection, be gentle, and always put them back where you found them.

Additional facts: A cool thing about reptile scales is they are made up of keratin, much like fingernails.

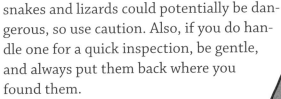

HUMMINGBIRDS ARE THE ONLY BIRDS THAT CAN FLY BACKWARD.

Bird flight is an impressive enough feat. But even more astounding is the fact that hummingbirds can fly backward. They can do this because instead of flapping their wings straight up and down like other birds, they pivot their wings in a figure-eight pattern. Flying backward is a pretty handy skill to have if you spend your life sticking a long, thin beak deep into flowers. Hummingbirds zip and dart around, but they are also one of the few birds that can hover in place. They can flap their wings up to sixty times per second. Go ahead and try to top that!

Hummingbirds are around the size of a golf ball, and they weigh about as much as a nickel.

70: Plants will only bloom once a season, and then they die.

MYTH SCALE: 2

About the myth: Summer is a very colorful time of year with all the flowers popping up everywhere. Sometimes it seems like you wait and wait and wait until that special flower bud finally opens to reveal a bloom. Then within days the show is over and you wait for another plant to perform instead.

The truth: It's easy to think plants only bloom and die, but this is not the case for all of them! Lots and lots of flowers will rebloom all summer. And there's a little something you can do to help them keep blooming. It's a funny little word called "deadheading." Whenever you see a bloom starting to fade, you should just go over and pluck it off. Now wait for it—pretty soon (a few days or a week or more) a new bloom will emerge and the show continues! You can't do this for all plants, but you can definitely try it with common ones like petunias, geraniums, pansies, and asters. It's a good way to keep your flowers looking great for even longer!

The takeaway: If you have a flower in your backyard, try to do a little research to figure out what it is. Then do an online search to see if it's a good one to deadhead. Or if you want a good flower to deadhead all summer, get a pack of petunias. They're inexpensive and really are pretty through fall.

Additional facts: Want a way to enjoy flowers for months? Take pictures of flowers! The morning is a perfect time to do this, especially if there's morning dew. Even if there's not morning dew, water your flowers in the morning and then take photos. It's cool if you can capture a droplet of water on camera!

71: Butterflies come from cocoons.

MYTH SCALE: 3

About the myth: Butterflies start off as caterpillars. And caterpillars transform into butterflies in cocoons right? Seems pretty clear. How is this even a myth?

The truth: It is almost as simple as that. Except butterflies don't make cocoons, they make chrysalises. Moths are the ones that make cocoons. It takes butterflies four stages to become adults: egg, larva, pupa, adult. Adult butterflies lay eggs on specific host plants. Caterpillars (the larva stage) emerge from the eggs, and then they eat. And they eat. And they eat. As caterpillars continue to eat, they outgrow their skin. They'll shed their skin multiple times. The final molting of skin is what forms the outer shell of the chrysalis (the pupa stage). The pupa stage lasts around a week or two for most butterflies. The transformation from caterpillar to adult butterfly is called metamorphosis. The chrysalis splits open and the adult butterfly emerges. After unfolding and drying the wings, it takes off for the first flight.

The takeaway: Metamorphosis happens for both butterflies and moths. Just remember that butterflies hatch out of chrysalises and moths from cocoons.

Additional facts: Metamorphosis is when an animal goes through a huge change in shape and structure during its lifetime. Insects aren't the only animals that can experience it. For example, tadpoles changing into frogs is also called metamorphosis.

72: Baby sea turtles hatch during the full moon.

MYTH SCALE: 2

About the myth: Baby sea turtles hatch out at night. Don't they need to have a full moon so they can find their way to the ocean?

The truth: Sea turtles hatch out of eggs on land, but they spend much of their lives at sea. The funny thing is, after the female comes to shore to lay her eggs, she heads right back out to the ocean. The eggs are left to incubate in the sand for a couple of months. Then when the babies hatch out, they are on their own. It is pretty crazy to think that baby sea turtles never see their parents. They do hatch out at night, but it doesn't have to be during the full moon. Hatching can be during any phase of the moon. Instinctively the young sea turtles head for the horizon that is more lit up. This should be toward the water, but with artificial lighting they can get turned around and head inland instead.

The takeaway: If you are walking along the beach at night, perhaps you'll be lucky enough to see the remarkable sight of baby sea turtles scrambling down the beach and off to sea. Even if it isn't on the night of a full moon.

Additional facts: All of the species of sea turtles found in North America are threatened or endangered.

AUTUMN

73: Bats are blind.

MYTH SCALE: 3

About the myth: Have you ever heard the saying "blind as a bat" before? These flying mammals are active under the cover of darkness, and it is nearly impossible for us to see anything in the dark. Seems likely that bats could be blind.

The truth: Bats don't rely on sight nearly as much as people do. That doesn't mean they are blind though. All bats can see. Some of the fruit-eating bats can see especially well. Bats that feed on insects have another adaptation to help them locate food. It's called echolocation and it is when bats send out high-pitched sounds and listen for the sounds to rebound off surrounding objects. Bats detect what is around them and pinpoint their insect meals this way. The echolocation sounds are too high-pitched for people to hear, but researchers can use special equipment to detect these signals. The scientists can even tell bat species apart based on their echolocation sounds.

The takeaway: Even though they are mostly nocturnal, bats are not blind. They have good vision but even better hearing. Maybe instead of "blind as a bat," the phrase should be "hear like a bat."

Additional facts: While we are on the subject of bats, let's talk about the whole rabies issue. Some people are convinced all bats have rabies. While bats can be carriers of rabies, they are no more or less susceptible than other mammals. As with all wild animals, give bats plenty of space. Especially if they are out during the day or they are acting strange in any other way.

74: Daddy longlegs are the most venomous spiders.

MYTH SCALE: 3

About the myth: With a plump body and long thin legs, daddy longlegs are easy to spot scampering daintily along. There is nothing to be afraid of, right? You've heard that they are the most venomous spiders in the world, but they can't bite a person. Their fangs are too small to break the skin of a human.

The truth: The short answer to this legend is "false." The long answer isn't much more complicated, but it does take a bit of explaining. First off, you need to clarify which daddy longlegs you are talking about. The name can refer to any of the species of harvestmen (technically, they aren't even spiders) or some species of cellar spiders. Neither of these groups are venomous to humans.

The takeaway: Harvestmen are scavengers that feed on plant and animal matter. They will also eat small insects. Cellar spiders also eat insects. But the bottom line is they aren't venomous to people. It is not true that they are the most venomous spiders out there.

Additional facts: Harvestmen tend to retreat from danger. The legs of harvestmen can even twitch after they are removed from the body. This might distract a potential predator while the harvestman escapes. Cellar spiders have been known to shake violently to try to scare off danger.

75: You can figure out a rattlesnake's age by counting its rattles.

MYTH SCALE: 2

About the myth: Rattlesnakes are fascinating creatures. They have many cool features, from the tips of their forked tongues to the last segments on their rattled tails. Bigger snakes have more individual rattle segments. But are they like tree rings? Can you count the segments to determine the age of the snake?

The truth: Rattlesnakes are one of the few snakes that give birth to live young. These baby snakes have a small rattle segment on the tip of the tail, called the prebutton. This is lost when the snake sheds for the first time and is replaced with a segment called the button. A new section of rattle is added each time the snake sheds, but snakes shed more than once per year. Rattles can break off sometimes, so counting the segments might not even give you the accurate count on the number of sheds.

The takeaway: As rattlesnakes shed their skin, new rattle segments are added to the tail. They can shed multiple times per year though, so counting these isn't helpful in determining the age of the snake.

Additional facts: Similar to fingernails, rattlesnake rattles are made up of keratin. There isn't anything inside the rattles, instead the sound is created when the segments vibrate off one another. Snakes can shake the tip of their tail up to sixty times per second to create the warning buzz.

76: Feeding birds in fall stops their migration.

MYTH SCALE: 3

About the myth: Some people say you should take down your bird feeders in the fall. The theory is that if birds can still find enough food, they won't migrate south before winter hits.

The truth: Migration is about finding food, but that doesn't mean if you provide food, the birds will stick around. It helps to understand a bit more about migration. Migratory birds experience a sort of restlessness known as Zugunruhe. Migration is triggered by photoperiod (the amount of sunlight each day). Migratory species head south as the days get shorter. Each bird species is different, and some don't ever migrate. You can always find some bird species all year long, even in the far north.

The takeaway: The migration cycle is something birds know naturally. Based on natural signals, including the length of the day, migratory birds fly between winter and summer homes. Feeding the birds during migration can help them fuel up for their journey, but it won't keep them from migrating onward. Birds will build up fat reserves before tackling the challenge of migration. Some species can nearly double in weight. This fat provides them the energy they need on these long-distance flights. It is like filling up your gas tank before a long road trip.

Additional facts: Some birds may use the earth's magnetic field to help them navigate, while others might use the night sky as a reference.

77: Hummingbirds migrate on the backs of swans or geese.

MYTH SCALE: 3

About the myth: There are many stories out there to explain where birds go in winter and how they get there. One of the more entertaining stories is that hummingbirds will hitch a ride on the backs of larger birds like geese to get where they need to go.

The truth: Sometimes smaller birds will chase larger birds, but this doesn't mean they are trying to get a ride. For one thing, geese and hummingbirds aren't usually found in the same types of habitats. Also, they migrate at different times, and they fly to different locations for the winter. This myth is just a bit of folklore that mistakenly gets passed around from time to time.

The takeaway: It is pretty incredible that something as tiny as a hummingbird can make an epic migration, but they do. Ruby-throated hummingbirds can even fly for 18 hours nonstop to get across the Gulf of Mexico to their wintering grounds. Not all hummingbirds have to migrate though. Anna's hummingbirds and other species in California and the Southwest aren't migratory at all.

Additional facts: Hummingbirds can flap their wings over sixty times per second! Go ahead and try to flap *your* "wings" that fast.

Luck Legends

THE WISHBONE CAN BRING YOU GOOD LUCK.

Have you ever pulled apart the wishbone from a Thanksgiving turkey? The wishbone (which is actually called the furcula) is right by the neck of a bird and has two pieces that comes to a center. Whenever you have the wishbone free, you're supposed to find a friend, both hold one side, and make a secret wish. Then you both pull, and whoever gets the largest part when it splits up will hopefully have his or her wish come true.

78: Flying squirrels can fly.
MYTH SCALE: 2

About the myth: When you think of animals that fly, you mostly think of birds, right? Maybe even insects, but what about mammals? Most mammals can't fly, but there are a few that can—like bats. What about flying squirrels though? They can fly, right? They are called *flying* squirrels after all.

The truth: Flying squirrels are small mammals that live in holes in trees (called cavities, just like holes in your teeth). They come out at night to feed. Despite their name, flying squirrels can't really fly. However, they do have remarkable adaptations that allow them to glide from tree to tree. Flying squirrels usually glide less than 20 feet. An impressive glide can go well over 100 feet, but no matter how hard they try, flying squirrels can't fly up.

The takeaway: Flying squirrels have flaps of skin between their front and back legs called patagium. A squirrel will climb high up in a tree and then jump off. The patagium acts like a parachute as the animal "flies" to another tree. The long tail acts like a rudder, so the squirrel can steer a bit.

Additional facts: North America has two species of flying squirrels. They look pretty similar but are found in different regions. Flying squirrels are active at night, so they have large eyes to help them see in the darkness.

Be a Scientist

COLLECT AND DRY YOUR OWN SEEDS

To grow new plants and veggies each spring, you could buy seeds or you could just save seeds in the fall instead. You can pretty much save seeds from every plant in the garden. Sure, some are trickier than others, but this is a fun and free way to test out your skills.

Supplies: Seed heads, paper bags, paper towels, string, recycled mint containers
Time: 10 minutes to gather seeds; a few weeks to a few months to let them dry
Observe and learn: To save the seeds, you have to figure out where the seeds are. Do you know where you'll find the seeds for fruits? What about vegetables? And flowers? The seeds can be hidden, so take a closer look to find the seeds.

How-To:
1. Find the seeds you want to save first. Fruit and veggie seeds are on the inside and can be taken straight from them as you eat. Flower seeds are usually hidden underneath or behind the flower. Once you know how to find the seeds, you'll know which method of saving seeds you need to use.
2. For the paper-bag method, you cut off entire stems of flowers in late summer or early fall, whenever the flower is pretty much done blooming. Then you tie a paper bag around the top and hang it upside down. As the flower dries, the seeds will naturally fall out.
3. For the paper-towel method, you place seeds on a paper towel and let them dry. You'll probably want to give them several weeks to dry completely.
4. Use little mint containers to store your seeds. Don't forget to keep them separated and label what you have. Store the seeds in a refrigerator or other dark and cool location. Then in spring, start seeds indoors or plant them directly in the ground.

You can even collect seeds from fruit like apples or oranges you buy from the store, but don't necessarily expect them to grow. Do it more for an experiment than anything.

Stranger than Fiction

SEA STARS CAN REGROW THEIR ARMS.

Sea stars (sometimes called starfish) are remarkable creatures of the ocean. They survive without brains and without blood. Instead, their nervous system is spread throughout their bodies, and they use seawater to pump nutrients through their system. These adaptations make it possible for sea stars to do another incredible thing: They regrow their arms! Most sea stars have five arms, but some species can have many more, like up to forty! In addition, many of these species can regrow an arm if one is damaged. The process takes a while, up to about a year. This regrown area will generally be weaker than before, but still, can you imagine being able to regrow an arm?

Some sea stars can extend their stomachs outside of their bodies to allow them to digest foods they can't fit inside their mouths.

79: Sharks have to swim to breathe.

MYTH SCALE: 2

About the myth: Sharks seem to be in constant motion. Are they looking for their next meal, or are they simply swimming to stay alive? Sharks breathe with gills, but if there isn't water flowing over their gills, they will die.

The truth: Sharks get the oxygen they need to survive when water passes over their gills. There are two different ways to make this happen. It's called buccal pumping and ram breathing (or ram ventilation). Buccal pumping is when the buccal muscles along the cheek force the water through the gills. Ram ventilation is when swimming forces the water through the mouth and over the gills. Very few species of sharks rely on ram breathing alone. Most can switch between the two types of breathing.

The takeaway: For a few species of sharks, including great white, mako, and whale sharks, swimming is the way to breathe. The majority of sharks can breathe without swimming. Some sharks spend lots of time settled along the ocean floor.

Additional facts: Whale sharks are the largest sharks, but they feed on some of the smallest ocean critters. Rare in the world of sharks, whale sharks are filter feeders, eating algae, plankton, and krill.

Weather Legends

IF OAK TREES STILL HAVE THEIR LEAVES IN OCTOBER, IT'S GOING TO BE A COLD WINTER.

First you need to find an oak tree. Then you need to observe it from the beginning to the end of October. Supposedly, if there are still leaves on late in the month, then it could be a cold winter. Of course, this really isn't the most scientific way to predict weather, but it is a fun reason to keep track of how long it takes oak trees to lose all their leaves.

80: Only male animals grow antlers.

MYTH SCALE: 1

About the myth: In the animal world males and females are sometimes called different things. For example, moose and elk males are called bulls and the females are called cows. It is buck (male) and doe (female) for deer. The easiest way to tell the males from the females is to look for antlers, right?

The truth: Antlers are bone-like structures that are grown annually. Every year they are shed off and then regrown. That means at certain times of the year neither males nor females have antlers. You can still see the pedestal where the antlers grow, though, if you look close. Also, female caribou (reindeer are technically the same thing) grow antlers. Female caribou antlers tend to be smaller than male antlers.

The takeaway: It is only the males that grow antlers in most species, but the one exception in North America is the caribou. It is extremely rare, but once in a while a female deer can grow antlers.

Additional facts: For all species, antlers grow quickly during the summer months. They are covered with blood vessels (called velvet) and have a soft, fuzzy appearance as they grow. Male antlers are important during the rut or breeding season. Large antlers can intimidate other males. There are also occasional pushing matches between two males to sort out disputes and to try to impress the females.

Stranger than Fiction

MOST BIRDS CAN'T STICK THEIR TONGUES OUT.

Sticking your tongue out is easy enough, but bird tongues are way different than mammal tongues. Instead of having thick, fleshy muscles, bird tongues are often thin and flat. Thin bones and cartilage support bird tongues. A few species of birds have very specialized tongues, especially woodpeckers and hummingbirds. Both of these types of birds can stick their tongues out incredibly far. This is quite rare in birds, but this adaptation helps these species eat. Woodpeckers flick their tongue under tree bark to eat hard-to-reach insects and larvae. Hummingbirds can stick their tongues deep into tube-shaped flowers as they feed on nectar. If you pay close attention, you can sometimes see woodpeckers and hummingbirds using their tongues at bird feeders.

Birds don't have lips! Instead they have beaks or bills.

81: All rats carry disease.

MYTH SCALE: 2

About the myth: Rats have long been blamed for eating field crops and stored grains. They are also blamed for many disease outbreaks including the famous Black Death of Europe in the 1300s. Some people are convinced the mere sight of a rat is almost certainly a death sentence. But how true is that?

The truth: Rats have gotten a bad rap over the years. There are a few illnesses that rats can transmit. This is true of most animals though. There are numerous species of "rats," and they aren't even all related to one another. Although they are now widespread across much of the world, two of the main species of city-dwelling rats aren't native to North America. They arrived via ships as early as the 1500s. The rats native to North America usually have less of a direct association with humans.

The takeaway: Some sicknesses that are blamed on rats don't come from them at all. For instance, plague comes from fleas and has nothing to do with rats. Rats, and rat droppings, can also spread some diseases, so take care if you are cleaning up areas that rats have been using. Don't worry—rats aren't any more dangerous than other wild animals.

Additional facts: Rats can cause problems in ecosystems where they aren't native, especially on islands. They are an added predator that can have a major impact on local plants and animals.

82: Opossums hang by their tails.

MYTH SCALE: 3

About the myth: Animals as different as monkeys, anteaters, tree porcupines, and lizards can hang from tree branches with their prehensile tails. Many marsupials also have this distinctive skill. Having a tail is cool enough, but being able to hang from a tail is a really awesome trick. But can opossums hang by their tails?

The truth: The opossum species found in the United States and southern parts of Canada is the Virginia opossum. While many species of opossum can have fully prehensile tails, adult Virginia opossums can't hang from their tails. Their bodies are too heavy and their tails are too weak. They can twist their tails around branches to use it like an extra leg. This helps them balance.

The takeaway: Virginia opossums can climb trees, but they can't hang by their tails. But that doesn't make them any less cool. They still have distinct marsupial adaptations, including a pouch. Young opossums are quite small when they are born. They stay in the pouch for two months as they continue to grow. Once they leave the pouch, young opossums sometimes can be seen riding along on their mother's back.

Additional facts: Opossums have a highly variable diet. They'll scavenge up almost anything to eat. For example, insects and worms . . . eggs and baby birds . . . plant matter . . . roadkill . . . even garbage. The habit of eating roadkill leads many opossums to unfortunately become roadkill themselves.

83: Lemmings will follow one another off cliffs to their death.

MYTH SCALE: 3

About the myth: It is said that lemmings will follow one another over cliffs, plunging to their death. Based on this, people who follow the crowd (i.e., don't think for themselves) are sometimes called lemmings. But is there any truth to this name-calling?

The truth: Lemmings are small mammals similar to mice. The populations of many species of lemmings can grow rapidly and then crash suddenly. Some years there are lemmings scurrying everywhere on the northern landscapes. Other years it can be hard to find a lemming anywhere. One of the theories to explain the disappearance of lemmings has been that they would plunge to a mass death over a cliff. This isn't true though. This concept has been popularized over the years in movies, television shows, and even a video game.

The takeaway: Lemmings, like most small mammals, have fairly short life spans. Lots of other critters would love to make a snack out of a lemming. But despite the claims, lemmings aren't following each other to their death.

Additional facts: At times in the 1500s, there were so many lemmings running around, people thought they must be falling from the sky or blown in with the strong winds.

84: You can tell how old an animal is by counting its antler points.

MYTH SCALE: 3

About the myth: Antlers come in many shapes and sizes. Antlers are impressive headgear. You can't really compare antlers from species to species. Elk have long thin tines, while moose have flatter antlers. Most things start off small and they get bigger and bigger as they grow up. Antlers could be that way too. They do fall off and grow back every year, so maybe animals grow one new antler point for every year of their lives.

The truth: The first set of antlers can be a single pair of spikes, and it is true that antlers can grow larger year after year. But some really old animals can have smaller antlers again. A lot of other factors go into antler growth too. Things like age but also genetics, disease, and animal nutrition.

The takeaway: You can't simply count the antler points to age an animal. If you find a skull to examine, ignore the antlers, and look at the teeth. Teeth wear down over the years, so you can get a rough estimate on the age of an animal by simply examining a jaw.

Additional facts: Horns are another structure grown on the heads of some animals, like bighorn sheep, bison, and cattle. Horns are made up of a bony core and covered in a keratin sheath. Unlike antlers that have multiple tines, horns don't branch.

Weather Legends

IF A ROOSTER CROWS AT NIGHT, THERE WILL BE RAIN BY THE NEXT MORNING.

Shouldn't roosters just crow in the morning? So what about when they start crowing at night? Some think this is suspicious activity, and when this happens there's going to be rain the next day. Ask someone who has a rooster what he or she thinks of this legend.

85: Beavers eat fish.

MYTH SCALE: 3

About the myth: Beavers are some of the most aquatic mammals. They spend much of their lives in and around water. Some of the best places to find fish can be in beaver ponds. Does that mean beavers eat fish?

The truth: Beavers don't eat fish. In fact, beavers often help create fish habitat. Beavers are nature's dam builders. By chewing down trees to block rivers and streams, beavers create deeper pools of water that many fish thrive in. Adding trees and branches to the underwater landscape can also help give fish added cover and protection from predators. Predators of fish can be mink, birds, and bigger fish, but beavers aren't fish predators.

The takeaway: Beavers are large rodents. Like most other rodents, beavers are herbivores, so they eat vegetation. For example, they'll graze on grasses and nibble on leaves during the spring and summer months. Beavers also eat the cambium layer of trees (between the bark and the wood). They also eat more bark and twigs that they've cached (stored) for the winter.

Additional facts: Beavers are adapted to aquatic life. They've got thick, heavy fur and special caster glands to help them keep this fur waterproof. Beavers have huge hind feet that are like webbed paddles. Their ears, eyes, and noses are high up on the head, allowing beavers to hear, see, and breathe while they swim along. They have a big, powerful tail that helps propel them along. When startled, a beaver will sometimes slap its tail on the surface of the water, creating a loud noise and a big splash!

Stranger than Fiction

IF OWLS WERE HUMAN SIZE, THEIR EYES WOULD BE SOFTBALL SIZE.

Owls have captivated people for centuries. Humans have something in common with owls: their large, forward-facing eyes. While most animals have eyes on the sides of their heads, owls don't. People don't either! These oversize eyes are stuck in place in the eye sockets, so owls have to move their heads to see around them. Having big eyes has its advantages. Great big eyes are helpful in judging distances, and they also help them to see in low-light conditions. Owls have other features that make them great night predators too. For instance, they have amazing hearing, sharp talons, and cool feathers that are called "barbless," making them silent fliers!

Some owls can rotate their talons around so they can get a better hold of their prey.

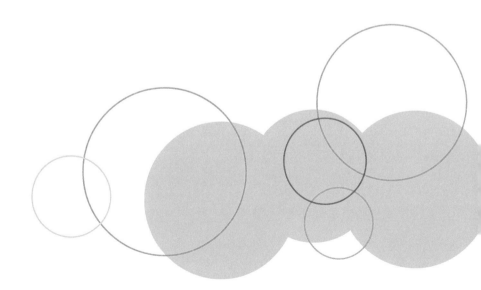

86: Owls are wise.

MYTH SCALE: 3

About the myth: The thought that owls are wise has been around for hundreds of years. From folklore to blockbuster movies, owls have often been used to depict intelligence and wisdom.

The truth: Owls are animals that seem to have a gaze when they are looking around. Owls aren't the only animals with eyes, but very few species have eyes that stare back at you like these species. The oversize, forward-facing owl eyes might have led to the false notion that these are the wisest of birds. This comes down to something called anthropomorphism. It's a big word, but it basically means you give human thoughts, feelings, and emotions to nonhuman things like animals. These are usually traits that humans can relate to or are often viewed positively. So it looks like people have been saying owls are wise without having much to back it up.

The takeaway: Measuring intelligence is tricky business. Owls are pretty great at being owls. Just because you can look into their big owl eyes doesn't make them smarter than hawks, eagles, warblers, or sparrows. It also doesn't make them any smarter than the mice or rabbits that they eat. It just makes them owls.

Additional facts: Owl eyes give them incredible vision, but the hearing of these hunters is even more impressive. The feathered tufts on some owls aren't ears. (They aren't horns either.) Owls don't have external ears, but what is really unusual is that their ears aren't directly opposite of each other. One ear opening is higher up on the side of the head and the other one is lower down. This helps owls pinpoint the exact location of a sound.

87: Clouds are white.

MYTH SCALE: 2

About the myth: This is an easy one. You go outside on a sunny day, look up, and see that the clouds that are in the sky are white. That's it—you're done. How can this be a real myth? You're seeing it with your own two eyes.

The truth: Here we go—it's one of those tricky ones where the colors are not really the colors you're seeing necessarily. They are just a reflection of sorts and seem to form a specific color, like white. So technically, the clouds are not white. However, put that aside for a second and think about clouds in general. On rainy days, how do the clouds look? Don't they seem dark and gray? What about on other days when the clouds almost seem to have a blue hue to them?

The takeaway: You can't have a blanket statement where you say all clouds are white. They might appear to be white (just like a rainbow appears to have seven colors—see the "Spring" section—but it's really a type of reflection more than anything.

Additional facts: *Psst!* Clouds aren't soft and fluffy either. They might look like giant puffy pillows that are soft and comfy, but that's just the way they are formed. Still, it's fun to imagine shapes in the clouds. Have you ever played a game of "I Spy" with clouds?

Luck Legends

IF YOU CATCH A FALLING LEAF ON THE FIRST DAY OF FALL, YOU'LL HAVE GOOD LUCK IN WINTER.

This one is an easy one to try. First off, you're going to have to find out when the first day of fall is. Then on that day, go outside for a walk where there are lots of trees. You can either walk around for a bit or sit under a tree waiting for a leaf to fall, but when one does, you better make sure you reach out and grab it. Whether or not this legend is true, it sure is fun to catch a leaf, especially on the first day of fall.

88: Male birds are brighter colored than females.

MYTH SCALE: 2

About the myth: Have you ever looked outside to see a bright-red cardinal perched on a branch? Keep looking and maybe you'll see a bird that looks like a cardinal nearby—except there's a big difference because it's not as colorful. It has some red on it, but it is not nearly as bright as the first one. You're looking at a male and a female cardinal. It must mean all male birds are brighter than the females, right?

The truth: In several cases, male birds really do have brighter feathers than the females. Examples of this include male ducks, cardinals, bluebirds, and lots of warblers. But this isn't always the case. In many instances, males and females look exactly the same. For example, blue jays, chickadees, titmice, and wrens all look alike. It's almost impossible to tell from a distance whether you're looking at a male or a female. In shorebirds called phalaropes, the females are brighter than the males.

The takeaway: Don't assume you're looking at a male! As you learn the birds in your own backyard and beyond, take the time to look them up and figure out if there are differences between males and females. It makes it a lot more fun when you spot one out in the wild.

Additional facts: Woodpeckers are a bit tricky. Some woodpecker species look exactly the same between male and female, and others have just small differences. It might be just a matter of one having a small red patch on the back of its head and the other not. Get a good field guide and see if you can pick out the differences between woodpeckers.

89: You need a big space to grow a veggie garden.
MYTH SCALE: 2

About the myth: When you plant vegetables in the spring, you don't think of them taking over the space in just a few short months. But that's often what happens. With all kinds of veggies that have vines going in every direction imaginable, bigger is always better when it comes to having a vegetable garden.

The truth: People have been pretty creative when it comes to growing their favorite veggies. Many people use different vertical methods, like using trellises and little plant ties so they grow their garden up instead of out. One of the most popular methods of growing veggies in small spaces is something called square-foot gardening. You can grow a good variety in just a few feet. Finally, you don't even have to have a whole space dedicated to growing veggies. Just tuck some plants where you already have flowers or shrubs growing, and they'll do just fine.

The takeaway: Be creative if you don't have a lot of space. Fall is a good time to look around to see where you might be able to tuck some veggie plants next year. You might be surprised at how easy it is to have a veggie garden in the space you already have.

Additional facts: Lots of people just grow things in pots or containers. So you don't even have to have a specific garden space. You can just put pots on a patio, deck, or balcony. As long as you have enough sunshine, your container garden should do just fine.

Be a Scientist

TAKE NATURE RUBBINGS

Don't just pass this off as an activity for little kids. It's a lot of fun to make nature prints with paper and crayons, no matter how old you are. You could even turn it into a game to see if you can guess what each print is.

Supplies: White paper, crayons, a clipboard
Time: 20 minutes
Observe and learn: Study the different textures in nature. Compare different leaves to see if some are smoother than others. Try to find unique objects and shapes that others might not notice.

How-To:

1. You can either do this experiment by hiking and then bringing the objects back to do a rubbing, or you can take your clipboard along with you and do the rubbings right there in the natural setting. So decide which way is right for you.
   You need to do a little preparation first. To get your crayons ready, you'll want to peel the paper off them.
2. As you're on your hike, you should look for both big and small items to do rubbings with. Once you find an item, place your paper on top of it. Then gently rub back and forth with your crayon on its side. As you rub, a print of your object should come through onto your paper.
3. If the print didn't come through well, try pressing a little harder on the crayon. A different color might show up better as well.
4. Once you have one print, go to the next object and make a print from it. Set a goal of collecting at least five to seven different prints. Then let everyone try to figure them out.

Be respectful of nature. It's OK to collect leaves or tree bark from the ground, but it's a good rule of thumb not to forcefully pull anything up, out, or off.

90: Flower bulbs are always planted in fall.

MYTH SCALE: 2

About the myth: If you go to a garden store in the fall, chances are you're going to see bags of bulbs everywhere. Tulips, daffodils, hyacinths—these are all bulbs you need to plant at this time of year if you want to have pretty flowers in spring. In fact, it's probably best to plant all of your bulbs in the fall.

The truth: This is another case where it varies by type. Many bulbs need a cold period in order to grow properly. This is why people plant bulbs in the fall. It offers a natural cold period because they'll be down in the ground when it freezes in winter. Then in spring when the ground thaws, the bulbs start to grow again. These are really just for those spring bulbs though. Be sure to check out your garden store again in spring, and you'll see a whole other grouping of bulbs that you can plant in spring for summer blooms.

The takeaway: If you want to grow tulips, daffodils, and those types, then yes, you will need to plant in fall. Either way, it's a good reason to hit up the garden store and do a little investigating. Challenge yourself to plant a bulb that you've never heard of this fall. Then go back and explore what bulbs you want to grow in spring.

Additional facts: Did you know garlic is a bulb? It's fun to grow. You just plant garlic bulbs in the ground much like you'd do with a daffodil or tulip. It also needs a cold period, so plant in the fall. Then when spring comes around, you'll be well on your way to having garlic.

91: Humans are the most abundant species on the planet.

MYTH SCALE: 3

About the myth: It's easy to think there are more humans on Earth than any other species. Think about it—you hear lots of stories on the news about how other animal populations are dying back. Yet the number of humans seems to keep growing and growing. We must be the most abundant species.

The truth: Humans aren't even close to being the most abundant species. Bugs far outnumber humans—specifically ants! In fact, humans come in at around seven billion while ants come in between one quadrillion and ten quadrillion. As a comparison, chickens come in at around sixteen billion. Can you believe chickens outnumber humans?

The takeaway: If you're just comparing large mammals, then yes, humans are one of the most abundant species. But they definitely aren't the largest species in total. As a comparison, the second-largest grouping of mammals is cattle, coming in at just over a billion.

Additional facts: Beetles also outnumber humans. They are the largest group of animals in the world because researchers estimate there are more than 300,000 different species out there, with new ones being discovered every year. Beetles are highly adaptable and can live in a lot of different conditions. This is why they thrive so much.

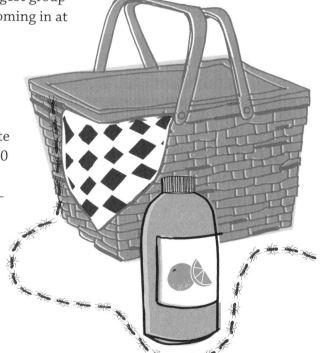

ARMADILLOS CAN JUMP HIGH.

Armadillos have thick, heavy skin that is almost scalelike. This forms scutes that are like strong armor protecting the armadillos from predators. It doesn't protect them from cars though. Unfortunately, many armadillos end up as roadkill each year. The nine-banded species is an armadillo that can jump up to 4 or 5 feet in the air when startled. This is a neat trick to scare off something that is trying to eat you, but it doesn't scare off cars. In addition to being great jumpers, armadillos are excellent in the water too. They can cross water by inflating their stomachs and intestines with air and floating along the surface of the water. They can also sink down to the bottom and use their sharp claws to walk along.

Armadillos can carry leprosy, a rare skin disease. In their defense, they probably caught the disease from humans first.

Weather Legends

IF YOU PUT AN ACORN ON YOUR WINDOWSILL, YOU CAN KEEP BAD WEATHER AWAY.

Now this one is a little bit tricky, and it's really not true. But it's a fun (and silly) thing to try if you're trying to avoid certain weather. For example, what is bad weather anyway? It probably differs a lot from one person to the next. It might mean rain to one person or snow to another. Even if this trick works for one day, chances are it won't keep a certain kind of weather away forever.

92: Clear water is safe to drink.

MYTH SCALE: 3

About the myth: It's easy to look at murky or dirty water and know that you probably don't want to drink it, right? So what about when you come across clear, beautiful water in the great outdoors? As long as it's clear, it should be OK to drink. Um, not so fast. Better keep reading!

The truth: You can't go by looks alone. A lot of water can be clear and look perfectly fine, but it could make you very sick because of what's inside. Most of the water that comes out of our faucets goes through a process to make it safe. So if you're out in the wild and come across some water that you want to drink, it's best to go through a process in that case too.

The takeaway: Even if water looks like it's coming from a fresh lake or stream, you shouldn't assume it's OK to drink. If you are planning to drink water out in the wild, it's best to go through a purification process. There are systems or tablets you can buy to make water out in the wild safe to drink. Do a little research on this if you're going to try it, but don't just drink water in the great outdoors without treating it first.

Additional facts: If you're camping and you need to use some water, but you're not sure about it being safe, boiling it is a good option.

93: Frogs *ribbit*.

MYTH SCALE: 2

About the myth: For years kids have been learning animal sounds, and the one long associated with frogs is the traditional *ribbit, ribbit, ribbit.* Movies, books, and all kinds of other media use the *ribbit, ribbit* sound of frogs in nearly everything they do, so it must be the sound that most frogs make.

The truth: First of all, there are a lot of different kinds of frogs out there, and there's no way they all make the same sound. Second of all, you'd probably be pretty surprised to hear the different kinds of sounds frogs can make. Chances are it's not what you're thinking. American bullfrogs have a very deep sound that doesn't sound like a *ribbit* at all. And many other frogs don't sound very froglike either. Now, the one frog that produces a sound most like a *ribbit* is the Pacific tree frog. This is probably where all those *ribbits* come from, but this is just one type of frog!

The takeaway: You can have a lot of different sounds when it comes to frogs. Take this opportunity to do some searching online to find out what frogs sound like. You could even put together a little test or quiz for your friends or parents to see if they can tell the differences between frogs. Now when you're out in the wild and you hear a funny noise, you might be able to identify it as a frog and teach others too.

Additional facts: We can probably blame Hollywood for the whole *ribbit, ribbit* thing. It makes sense. The Pacific tree frog is found all along California, where lots of movies and TV shows are made. So it's only natural that people there use it for the frog sounds.

94: All trees lose their leaves.

MYTH SCALE: 2

About the myth: It's autumn, which means leaves are starting to fade away. Soon they'll all be on the ground and we'll have bare trees for winter before we start seeing new growth next spring.

The truth: Think about the trees you see in your area for a minute. While everyone has different types of trees around them, one thing is probably similar—not all trees have leaves. For instance, pine trees don't have leaves at all. They have needles! And they don't lose all their needles in the fall like some trees do. The trees that lose their leaves in fall are called deciduous. Those that don't are called coniferous or evergreens.

The takeaway: Pay attention to the trees around you this time of year and then later again during winter. It's fun to start noticing which trees have leaves year-round and which do not.

Additional facts: So how do trees know when it's autumn and it's time to start losing their leaves? It has a lot to do with the weather. When temperatures start dropping, especially during the night, the leaves start to fall. So trees in northern areas, where it's colder, start losing leaves much earlier in the year.

Luck Legends

IF A BLACK CAT CROSSES IN FRONT OF YOU, YOU'LL HAVE BAD LUCK.

This legend has been around for a long time, but it's especially popular around Halloween. Black cats have long been associated with witches and evil things, but you should be fine unless one crosses in front of you. If it does, you better watch out because you never know what will happen.

95: All flowers smell.

MYTH SCALE: 2

About the myth: You know the phrase "Stop and smell the flowers"? Well, the phrase is really about taking the time to enjoy what's around you, but it also reminds us that all flowers have a scent so we should enjoy them every chance we get.

The truth: Sure, most things have some sort of scent, but not all flowers have that sweet, wonderful smell that a lot of people associate with flowers. There are basically two reasons for this. First, some flowers just don't smell, or if they do, the scent is very faint. Second, other flowers have lost their scent over the years because of the way plant people breed flowers. Basically, this means that some people developed plants to have other characteristics besides scent. The rose is the most classic example of this. Roses traditionally have lots of thorns and can be difficult to grow. So plant breeders have tried to make them easier to grow and to lose some of the thorns. But you can't have everything, and some of these changes have led to roses losing their wonderful smells.

The takeaway: You should just know that all blooms don't necessarily smell. Go up to flowers and put them to the test for yourself. You could even have a little bit of fun and make a chart. Go through the garden and rate what flowers smell best to you.

Additional facts: Some roses do still have wonderful sweet smells. See if you can find a rose grower or a rose garden in your area. Test out the roses and see if you can detect differences among them.

Be a Scientist

MAKE A TORNADO

You don't want to see a tornado up close, so make one in a jar instead. It's a safe and fun way to see how a funnel forms and then twists and turns, destroying most everything in its path.

Supplies: Glass jar and lid or 2 empty 2-liter bottles, water, dish soap, vinegar, duct tape, glitter

Time: 15 minutes

Observe and learn: One of the biggest reasons tornadoes are so destructive is because as they spin and rotate, no one knows which direction they're going to go. As you make your own tornado, notice how everything gets tossed all around.

How-To:

1. You can make a tornado a couple of different ways. For the first way, just take a clear glass jar with a lid. Make sure it's cleaned out, and then fill it about half to three-quarters of the way full of water. Then add about a teaspoon each of vinegar and dish soap. Before you put the lid on, add a little bit of glitter.

2. Make sure the lid is on tight and then start swirling it around. If you shake it fast enough and in a fluid rotating motion, you should see a funnel start to appear. The faster and stronger you move it, the better funnel you'll get.

3. In the second way of making a tornado, you'll take two two-liter bottles and seal them tightly together by the small openings. You don't do that just yet though.

4. First you need to put your water, vinegar, and dish soap inside the bottles. And don't forget to add a little bit of glitter. Again, you'll fill one bottle about one-half to three-quarters of the way full.

5. Now use duct tape to secure the bottles together. It's going to be near impossible not to have any leaks, but try to seal it as much as possible.
6. Then quickly turn the bottle with the water in it upside-down and swirl it in a circular motion as quickly as possible. The water should start to swirl into a funnel. As the tornado dies down, it'll slowly make its way into the bottom bottle. Then you just flip it and go again.

You can also buy a bottle connector that will help this project. Then you don't have to mess with duct tape or any leaks.

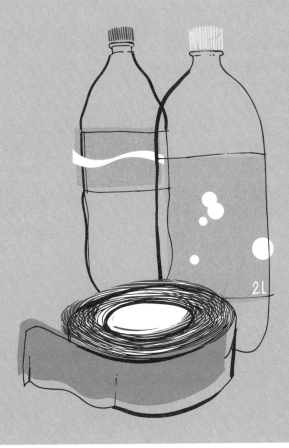

96: Baby animals are fuzzy.

MYTH SCALE: 2

About the myth: If you've ever held a little kitten or puppy, then you know they are just about the softest and fluffiest things imaginable. You just want to cuddle them as much as possible because they are so nice to touch. Other baby animals like rabbits and even baby birds must be just as fuzzy.

The truth: Are you ready to never think of baby animals the same again? OK—most baby animals are born just like you are: totally, 100 percent naked! So a lot of them start off with hardly any hair on their bodies at all. Or if they have some hair on their bodies, it's just small little bits, and it's certainly not what you would call fuzzy. For animals that have fur (or even feathers when it comes to birds), it takes a while for them to completely fill in and get that soft animal fuzz that you're thinking of. And then think about other baby animals like reptiles, frogs, and so on. When is the last time you heard someone talk about a frog being soft, fuzzy, and cuddly? No way!

The takeaway: Even baby animals that do have fur don't start off that way. Check out a book about baby animals in the nonfiction section of your library. Then you can see for yourself through a few pictures.

Additional facts: Have you ever held a baby chick or a baby duck? They are just about the softest animals you can find. While they grow up to develop large feathers that really aren't cuddly at all, it sure is fun to hold them when they're little.

TARANTULA VENOM IS WEAKER THAN BEE STINGS.

Tarantulas can be found in many parts of the world, although in the United States their range is limited to the southern states. Even though they are often used in scary movies, tarantulas are fairly harmless. Some people even keep them as pets. They do have mild venom, but it's the bite that will hurt the most. Have you ever noticed the hairs on tarantulas? They are special, called urticating hairs, and they can cause minor irritation if they get on the skin or in the eyes of predators. Here's another fun fact about tarantulas: They don't use a web to catch their prey. Instead they use their long legs to grab them. Then they paralyze their prey (usually insects but sometimes small lizards) with venom.

While the tarantulas of North America are mostly brown or black, in other parts of the world, they can be bright colored, including blue, yellow, or orange.

97: Starfish and jellyfish are both types of fish.

MYTH SCALE: 3

About the myth: Starfish and jellyfish—they both have *fish* in their name. Even though they're a little different than a lot of the typical fish you know, they have to be some type of fish, right?

The truth: A lot of people will tell you that starfish and jellyfish are actually the wrong names and you shouldn't be using them. They will tell you to instead use the terms "sea star" and "sea jelly." This is because they aren't really fish at all! They are actually more closely related to sea creatures like sand dollars and sea urchins. Starfish, for example, don't have gills, scales, or fins. And while jellyfish float around in the water more like fish do, they are made up quite differently as well.

The takeaway: Names can easily fool people, and in this case, it's not hard to see why. Starfish and jellyfish might have *fish* in their names, but they aren't types of fish at all.

Additional facts: The sea stars that you are probably familiar with are part of a family called the echinoderms. This is the same family to which sea dollars belong. (A lot of people don't realize sea dollars are animals. They think they are just shells.) Go ahead and surprise your friends and the adults in your life with that one!

98: A duck's quack doesn't echo.

MYTH SCALE: 3

About the myth: It's one of the most mysterious claims out there—a duck's quack doesn't echo. No one really knows why exactly, but the way the myth is told is that a duck's quack will not echo, no matter what the conditions are.

The truth: The claim that a duck's quack won't echo is really just silly. If in the right conditions, all sounds echo. It makes no sense that a duck noise would be any different. And because this myth is one that continues to be circulated again and again, several people have tested it for themselves. And in all the tests, the results are the same. A duck's quack does in fact echo.

The takeaway: This myth is completely debunked! If you want to test this one for yourself, it would be easy enough to do. Just get a duck recording, and then take it to a place where you know there's an echo. For instance, under a bridge or in a tunnel would work great. Then just hit the Play button.

Additional facts: Here's a fun fact about ducks that you might not know. Have you ever seen a duck out in very cold or even icy water? How can they stand those cold temperatures on their feet? Their veins and arteries are wrapped around each other, so this helps keep their blood (and their feet) from loosing too much heat.

99: All rocks sink in water.

MYTH SCALE: 2

About the myth: Rocks are often heavy, there's no doubt about that. And when you take one and try to skip it across the water, it might skip a couple of times, but then it sinks to the bottom. So of course all rocks sink. When is the last time you saw a rock floating in the water?

The truth: Wait just a minute there. While most are heavy and quickly fall to the bottom of a lake, pond, river, or ocean, a lot of that really depends on what the rock is made of. Then what about rocks that are just small in size? They won't necessarily just sink down to the bottom either. It looks like it's time to do a little experimenting so you can test this one out for yourself.

The takeaway: Whether a rock sinks or not depends on its size and the kind of material it's made out of. Gather up a variety of rocks to try this out. You're going to want all different sizes, and then try to find ones made of different materials too. For instance, sandstone is a lightweight material, so you might come across a larger sandstone rock that actually floats while a smaller rock made from a different kind of material will sink right away. Lava rock, called pumice, is another kind of rock that can sometimes float.

Additional facts: If you want to try skipping rocks, not all rocks are created equal. You want one that isn't too heavy or fat but instead is flat and has a nice curve to it. This way it'll just glide through the air and across the water. But once you have the perfect rock, your work is not done. It's all in getting the flick of the wrist just right.

KILLER WHALES ARE DOLPHINS.

Orcas are sometimes called killer whales, but get this—they aren't actually whales at all. Instead, they are more closely related to dolphins. Orcas are the largest dolphins, and sometimes they will even eat small whales. Having 4-inch-long teeth, they are excellent hunters (this is in part where the nickname "killer whale" came from). They will sometimes hunt in groups called pods and will eat fish, squid, seabirds, and marine mammals like seals and sea lions. On average, orcas live between fifty and eighty years in the wild. They grow up to 32 feet in length and can weigh as much as 6 tons. Orcas have complex social structures made up of closely related family units. More research needs to be done still, but scientists think there might be more than one species of killer whale.

Like other dolphins and whales, orcas communicate underwater using various sounds and clicks. They also use echolocation to communicate and hunt.

100: Cows have four stomachs.

MYTH SCALE: 3

About the myth: Cows are usually eating all day long. How do they have so much room for all that grass? Rumor has it that they have four stomachs. It makes sense. After all, their stomach area does seem pretty large.

The truth: Yes, cows have four of something, but it's not four stomachs. They have one stomach, but here's where it gets tricky—they do actually have four chambers in their stomachs! Think of these as four different compartments of sorts. The material they eat does actually pass through all four areas during the digestion process.

The takeaway: Don't let your friends trick you on this one. In fact, you could try tricking your friends. Cows do not have four stomachs, but their stomach does have four chambers. Look up a diagram online to see how this breaks down.

Additional facts: So what else do cows eat besides grass? They are mostly plant eaters, so they like grasses and hay. They also love fruit and will snack on apples, pears, and more.

MOST OF EARTH IS COVERED IN WATER.

Humans are terrestrial beings. Sure we like to swim in the water from time to time, but overall, land is essential for our survival. Most of our food comes from the land, so it might surprise you to know there's a lot more water than land around. As seen from space, the oceans are the most obvious feature of Earth. In fact, 70 percent of the planet's surface is covered in water. The vast majority of this water is salt water. Freshwater is also essential for humans, but just 3 percent of the water on the Blue Planet is freshwater. And get this: Most of that 3 percent is in ice caps and glaciers.

The first Earth Day was celebrated in 1970.

101: All birds can fly.

MYTH SCALE: 1

About the myth: Birds fly. It's just what they do. It doesn't get much simpler than that.

The truth: Most birds do fly, but there are a few exceptions. Penguins and ostriches are two exceptions to the "birds can fly" rule. Both of these birds can't fly at all, yet they are still birds. Other birds that cause a lot of confusion regarding whether they can fly are chickens and even turkeys. You usually see these birds grounded, but they can fly if they want to. Turkeys spend the night roosting in the tops of trees. They might not go great distances, but they still have what it takes to fly.

The takeaway: See if you can dazzle your friends with the fact that not all birds fly. It's one of those trickier ones because most do in fact fly. But you'll look even more impressive when you can tell them exactly which ones can't.

Additional facts: For birds that migrate in the fall, you might be surprised to find out that many young birds are all on their own! Yep, their parents aren't necessarily showing them where to go or fly. They have to figure it out all on their own even though they've never done it. So for birds that migrate hundreds of miles to the tropics for winter, they are figuring out how to get there without any help!

Be a Scientist

MAKE YOUR OWN SLIME

You can find a lot of things in nature that are similar to slime. For instance, mud and quicksand both have a slimy consistency. With this simple recipe, you can replicate the slime you find outside. There's just one rule: Don't eat either the stuff you find outside or the stuff you make inside!

Supplies: Cornstarch, water, food coloring, plastic storage containers
Time: 15 minutes
Observe and learn: You're going to want to make your slime nice and slow, feeling how the consistency changes with every little addition of water. Try to think of fun words to describe how it feels and see if everyone agrees.

How-To:
1. Use an entire box of cornstarch but divide it into separate bowls, depending on how many people you have. One box of cornstarch is probably enough for two to three people to make slime.
2. Have everyone really feel the cornstarch. How does it feel different than sugar or flour? Once everyone gets a good feel for it, start adding water, about half a cup at a time.
3. Each time you add water, have everyone mix the cornstarch with their hands. It'll be pretty thick at first, but as you mix it, it will start to have more of a runny consistency. Be careful not to add too much water. You want it to be a little stiff to the touch.
4. Once you have your slime at a good consistency, go ahead and add food coloring to it, making it whatever color you want. You can experiment with colors (as described in "Be a Scientist" in the "Winter" section).
5. After you're done playing with your slime, store it in a plastic container. Don't forget to compare it to the slime-like material you find in nature too. Get outside and get those hands dirty!

Another way to make slime involves using white school glue and borax, which you can find in the laundry aisle. See how it compares in texture to this slime.

102: All oak trees have acorns.

MYTH SCALE: 2

About the myth: Acorns come from oak trees. If you're going out on an acorn hunt, all you have to do is find an oak tree, and then you'll easily find a few acorns along the ground underneath the tree.

The truth: Yes, acorns do come from oak trees. And yes, pretty much all oak trees will have acorns. But you shouldn't expect to find acorns at all oak trees. Wait a minute now! Why not? It turns out that it can take quite a while for an oak tree to produce acorns. Some will produce them as early as 20 years of age, while others won't start producing them for fifty years or more. So if you're looking for acorns under an oak tree but are not finding any, maybe it's just a younger tree. If that's not the case, then check the season. Generally, acorns are produced in fall.

The takeaway: If you are looking for acorns, then you need to be on the lookout during fall, and you should be looking under mature trees. The older a tree is, the more acorns you're going to find!

Additional facts: How do you find an oak tree to begin with? There are hundreds of different types of oak trees out there, and they don't all look the same. So the best thing to do is start by figuring out what the leaves look like. Once you know how to identify the oak trees in your area by their leaves, you'll easily be on the road to finding acorns.

Weather Legends

Rings around the moon (some people also call them halos) are created by light passing through high, thin clouds. In fact, it's kind of like a rainbow because it's created in a similar way. It doesn't really indicate a certain kind of weather, but it's still something cool that you might want to keep an eye out for.

103: All woodpeckers peck wood.

MYTH SCALE: 2

About the myth: When it comes to woodpeckers, you just have to look at their name to understand them. The first part is *wood*. The second part is *pecker*. So they must peck wood. It's part of their name after all.

The truth: There is some truth to woodpeckers pecking wood, but do you know why they do it? There are a few reasons. First, they'll peck at wood to get at the insects hiding behind the bark. They'll also peck wood to carve out (also called excavate) a hole so they can nest there. And they will peck at wood to hide (also called cache) their food. But do all woodpeckers peck wood? No! In fact, some woodpeckers will peck at cacti instead.

The takeaway: Not all species of woodpeckers peck wood, but many do. There is a difference between holes that are carved out for nesting versus those for digging for insects or hiding food. Go on a hike to see if you can find a few holes in the trees that look like they came from a woodpecker.

Additional facts: Related to woodpeckers are a group of birds called sapsuckers. No, they don't necessarily suck up sap—don't be fooled by their name! Instead, they tap rows of sap wells into trees and then they dip their tongues into the sap that oozes out.

Stranger than Fiction

BEAVERS' TEETH NEVER STOP GROWING.

The beaver is the largest rodent in North America. They hang out near water and are most active at night. Even if you've never seen a beaver, maybe you've seen a tree stump that was chewed down to make a dam or a lodge. Beavers, like all rodents (including mice, chipmunks, and squirrels), have relatively long and sharp front teeth. These four incisors (two upper and two lower teeth) grow during the entire life of the animal. So why don't rodents all have tusks sticking out of their mouths? Most rodents eat seeds and other hard things. The beaver is always chewing on wood. This is like sandpaper and wears teeth down. To help protect against this wear, rodent teeth have extra enamel and they grow continuously.

The term "rodent" comes from the Latin word for gnawing, *rodere*.

104: All animals naturally have the ability to swim.

MYTH SCALE: 2

About the myth: A lot of swimming has to do with instinct. Have you ever seen dogs go in the water? Somehow they seem to just know to wiggle their front legs and swim to shore. After all, it's not called the dog paddle for nothing!

The truth: For the most part, animals are pretty good swimmers. A lot of animals are even able to swim within hours of being born. Not all animals have these same instincts though. For instance, people, apes, and chimpanzees have to learn how to swim. Did you learn how to swim? Do you remember how long it took? It's no easy task!

The takeaway: Swimming abilities differ from one animal to the next. If you happen to be at the zoo or somewhere in the wild where you see animals swimming, take a look at their different styles. Observe how some species differ from others.

Additional facts: All ducks are great swimmers, with their webbed feet, and wood ducks are some of the most impressive. A wood duck will jump out of its nest from high up in a tree within just a few hours of being born. Now that's impressive!

Luck Legends

IF YOU KNOCK ON WOOD, YOU CAN AVOID EVIL THINGS.

Here's how it goes: When you talk about something out loud that you don't want to happen, you're supposed to give a little "knock on wood" to ensure that it doesn't. For example, if you say something about how glad you are the dark-looking clouds haven't produced any rain yet, this legend says adding a little knock will help keep it that way. Without the knock? Well, then the odds just got worse!

105: Millipedes have 1,000 legs.

MYTH SCALE: 3

About the myth: Haven't you ever heard of "the 1,000-legged critter"? This refers to millipedes. If you've ever seen a picture of them, it's easy to see that they have a lot of legs—so the nickname must be right.

The truth: The name is part of the reason the myth about this bug keeps going— *milli* means thousand and *ped* means foot. So it translates to 1,000 feet. It's not true though! Yes, millipedes do have a lot of little legs, but not anywhere close to 1,000. Scientists say that most of them have fewer than one hundred legs. In fact, when they are first born, they only have three pairs of legs.

The takeaway: Just because they have a tricky name doesn't mean these bugs have 1,000 legs. The number of legs each one has can vary, but it's certainly not 1,000. Millipedes generally have two pairs of legs per body segement, while centipedes have one pair of legs per body segment.

Additional facts: Millipedes are considered an arthropod, and they are one of the longest-living insects in this category. They usually lay pretty low, and they can easily live five to seven years.

106: Animals sleep with their eyes closed.

MYTH SCALE: 2

About the myth: When you go to sleep, you close your eyes. This function seems pretty common and well known. How else are you supposed to sleep?

The truth: Animal sleep is fascinating. If you ever get the chance to check out a book about animal sleep from the library, you'll learn all kinds of things! But no, not all animals close their eyes when they sleep like we humans do. Lots of birds and fish sleep with their eyes open.

The takeaway: Sleep varies a great deal from one animal to the next. Some sleep standing up. Some sleep during the day. Some even sleep with their eyes open. But one thing is similar—all animals need sleep!

Additional facts: Dolphins are one of the most fascinating sleepers. They actually sleep with one eye open and continue to swim while they're sleeping! They will put part of their brain to rest while closing just one eye at the same time. It's pretty impressive.

Stranger than Fiction

FISH DON'T HAVE EYELIDS, BUT SHARKS DO.

Even though they both swim around in the water, sharks and fish don't have much in common. The reason they are so different is that they aren't closely related. Sharks belong to a different scientific class than other fish. These groups are called cartilaginous fish (which include sharks, rays, and chimeras) and bony fish. The most fundamental difference between the groups is that cartilaginous fish have a skeleton made of cartilage, while bony fish have a skeleton made of bone. Eyelids are another difference between the groups. Bony fish lack eyelids, while sharks have eyelids. Sharks even have a nictitating membrane, like a bonus eyelid, to help protect their eyes. Some shark species, including great white sharks, even have the incredible ability to roll their eyes back into the socket. Here's one more notable difference worth mentioning: Fish can swim backward, but sharks can't.

It is a myth that sharks don't get cancer.

107: All berries are poisonous.

MYTH SCALE: 2

About the myth: Be aware of any berries you see growing in the wild. If you eat them, they could make you very sick because they are probably poisonous.

The truth: You can't really label all berries as being poisonous. You can find plenty of wild berries that are edible, including wild blueberries, raspberries, mulberries, and even strawberries. However, if you're unsure about a specific berry, the best thing to do is leave it alone! Some berries that are considered poisonous would just make you feel a little queasy, while others could make you very ill. This is another case where it's better to be safe than sorry.

The takeaway: You can find some berries out there that are OK to eat, but you'd better be sure about what you're searching for first. If you're interested in finding berries in the wild to try, go with someone who knows for sure what he or she is looking for. You might even be able to find a wild-foraging class for your area. If you're unsure about anything, don't chance it—not even a small taste.

Additional facts: Did you know berries are a major food source for birds? They love them and especially rely on them in fall and winter. Try to plant some trees or shrubs that have berries in your yard to lure in as many birds as possible.

108: A dog's mouth is cleaner than a human's.

MYTH SCALE: 3

About the myth: It's one of those sayings that have been passed around for years. Humans have dirty, icky mouths and dogs are much, much cleaner. Some say they are even ten times cleaner!

The truth: Think about this one for a second. Have you ever seen what a dog will eat and lick? Take a dog outside for a little bit, and it will lick just about everything it sees, including dirt, rocks, sticks, and more. Now think about yourself for a second—you don't tend to lick things other than ice-cream cones, right? And you do brush your teeth pretty regularly, don't you? There's no way a dog's mouth is cleaner than yours. Experts say they think it got started because of the way dogs lick their wounds, which in turn seems to help them heal faster. From this it was assumed they must have a very clean mouth.

The takeaway: You can't say a dog's mouth is cleaner than a human's. It just isn't true. Go ahead and take a while to observe a dog and watch where it goes and where it puts its mouth. This might make you rethink a few things when it starts licking you next!

Additional facts: Here's a fun fact about dogs that makes them a bit similar to us. They dream! Yep, when you see a dog wiggling its paws or tail or whimpering while it's asleep, it might actually be dreaming!

MONARCHS MIGRATE FOR WINTER.

Where do butterflies go for winter? Most spend the winter in life stages other than adult butterflies. Many survive the cold in egg form, hatching out in the spring. A few survive in a suspended state as a chrysalis. A few species can overwinter as adult butterflies. The butterflies go into a hibernation-like state generally, but on especially warm days they might become active.

The monarch butterfly takes an approach out of the playbook of birds, as this species migrates south for the winter. Monarchs are large, powerful butterflies. One marked individual flew over 250 miles in one day, but most tend to stop more frequently than that. Not all monarchs migrate though. Each summer produces four or five generations of monarchs. Only the latest generations make the migration journey to wintering ranges in California and Mexico.

Monarchs prefer to lay their eggs on milkweed plants.

WINTER

109: The North Star is the brightest star in the sky.
MYTH SCALE: 3

About the myth: The North Star is also called Polaris. It's easy to assume that it's the brightest star in the sky because the whole northern night sky moves around it. You can usually pick it out because it's bright. At first glance it definitely looks like it could be the brightest star in the sky.

The truth: When it comes down to it, Polaris isn't even close to being the brightest star in the sky! Scientists have estimated that it ranks about fiftieth in brightness. So why is it so famous? Think about the earlier fact— the whole northern sky moves around it. This is pretty impressive. The Big Dipper and all the other stars in the area move around the North Star.

The takeaway: Don't assume that the bright star you're looking at in the sky is definitely the North Star. As you've learned, there are about forty-nine other stars that are even brighter! Instead, there's a better trick for locating the North Star, and it has to do with the Big Dipper. Want to know more? Keep reading!

Additional facts: Want to know how to find the North Star? First you need to be able to locate the Big Dipper constellation. Look up into the sky and notice how the Big Dipper looks like it's upside down. The two stars that make up the pot edge farthest from the handle point straight to the North Star. This is a good trick to learn, because once you know how to locate the North Star, you'll always know your way at night.

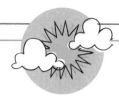

Weather Legends

OWLS HOOT MORE AT NIGHT IF RAIN IS ON THE WAY.

Here's another one that would be almost impossible to prove. First of all, you'll have to know how much the owls around you hoot regularly. Once you have that established, you'd be able to know if they are hooting more or less. But to tie their hooting to the rain? That's a tricky one! Just use this legend as an excuse to know what owl hoots sound like. Figure out what owls are in your area, and then look up online how they sound. (They probably don't sound like you think they do.) Now you know what to listen for!

110: You can rub snow on your skin to treat hypothermia.

MYTH SCALE: 3

About the myth: This myth is popular among hikers and mountain climbers. If you're out when it's cold and you can tell you're starting to get hypothermia, then you should just reach for some snow.

The truth: Hypothermia occurs when your body temperature drops for a long period of time. This can actually be really dangerous, leading to frostbite, which could result in losing toes, fingers, or other body parts. So it makes no sense to add more cold and ice to body parts that are already freezing! Instead, you'll want to warm up those areas so they can recover. Some people think that rubbing the cold area will create heat from friction, but this can cause serious damage to the body too.

The takeaway: Do not add snow, ice, or other cold things to areas where you're already cold. This is just silly. It's not going to make you feel warmer or stop hypothermia. If you're playing outside and are really cold, then just take a break. Use it as an excuse to head inside and have some hot chocolate.

Additional facts: You want a trick to keeping your hands and feet warm on cold days? First of all, you'll want to wear a couple of layers of socks and gloves. But also, you'll want to keep everything dry. Some wool clothes will also help keep you warm. It is way better at keeping you warm than cotton, especially if you get a little wet.

111: Groundhogs can predict the weather.

MYTH SCALE: 3

About the myth: Groundhogs have been predicting the weather for years. The way the story goes is that a groundhog comes out of its burrow and looks for its shadow. If it sees its shadow, it goes back inside, and we will have six more weeks of winter. If it doesn't, because it's a cloudy day, it stays outside, and that means spring is just around the corner!

The truth: This folklore dates back to the 1800s by the Pennsylvania Germans. It originates from Europe, where history says they would often use a badger instead of a groundhog to predict the weather. While lots of people look to animals to be weather predictors, this one doesn't have much credibility. You can't plan for six weeks of weather based on a single day of whether or not it's cloudy.

The takeaway: You don't need to believe the groundhog, but it's still fun to join in the celebration. Groundhog Day is on February 2 every year, and lots of people treat it like a holiday. People often hope for a cloudy day because by early February, they're sick of winter and would like an early spring.

Additional facts: Groundhogs are a type of rodent, and some people also refer to them as woodchucks. They are a type of ground squirrel, mostly found in the eastern half of the United States but also extend into Canada and parts of Alaska. They have powerful claws that are perfect for digging their burrows, where they sleep, raise their young, and hibernate for winter.

SWANS HAVE MORE THAN 25,000 FEATHERS.

Feathers are the most obvious feature that separates birds from all other animals. Surprisingly durable, feathers assist in flight, help birds maintain their body temperature, and can be useful in displays or as camouflage. Despite being lightweight, feathers can weigh more than the entire skeleton of a bird. Hummingbirds have around 1,000 feathers, while swans can have more than 25,000 feathers. Birds have numerous different kinds of feathers: the long flight feathers of the wings and tail, contour feathers along the body, fluffy down and semiplume feathers below the contour feathers, and specialized bristles around the eyes, nostrils, and mouth. Most birds molt (grow new feathers) during late summer, although some species molt in the springtime.

Individual flight and contour feathers are made up of a bunch of barbs attached to a central shaft. These barbs have barbules that fit together like Velcro, adding to the durability of the feathers.

112: You can't get sunburned on a cloudy day.

MYTH SCALE: 3

About the myth: Sunscreen is absolutely essential in the summer. It's so easy to get sunburned on bright, sunny days. But when it comes to cloudy days and winter in general, you really don't need to bother with it.

The truth: Stop right there! Every doctor will tell you that you can in fact get sunburned on cloudy days. And you can get sunburned any time of the year too! The thing is, most people don't spend as much time outside during the winter, so they might not be out long enough to get burned. Don't be fooled though! Those rays can still shine through the clouds and damage your skin. Just ask anyone who loves to go out skiing, sledding, or snowboarding. They'll tell you the sun still beats down no matter how many clouds are in the sky.

The takeaway: The sun is a very powerful thing and can do a lot of damage if you don't protect yourself against it. If you're going to be outside for a while, no matter what time of year it is, it's best to put sunscreen on.

Additional facts: Don't forget those lips! Have you ever had your lips burned? It's no fun! It's especially easy to get lip burn in the winter as you're zooming down the hill on your sled. Find a lip balm that has SPF in it, and you'll be glad you did!

Luck Legends

WEIRD THINGS HAPPEN ON NIGHTS OF A FULL MOON.

A lot of people swear by this legend. Some of the things that are supposed to happen during a full moon include more crime, more babies being born, and more accidents. While studies have shown that there's not really a correlation between these things and a full moon, many people still think there's a strong tie. No matter what you believe, everyone can agree that full moons are beautiful!

Stranger than Fiction

IF YOU LICK A FLAGPOLE, YOUR TONGUE WILL STICK TO IT.
There's a popular holiday movie called *A Christmas Story* where a kid is dared to stick his tongue on a metal flagpole. As soon as he does, his tongue sticks and he can't get it off! Though this happened in the movie, many people have challenged this and wondered if it's true. It absolutely is! If it's below freezing and you put your warm tongue on a metal object outside (or other items too), it very well could stick to it. It's a combination of the freezing temperatures with your warm body and wet tongue. It is a bad idea. And chances are it'll rip a piece of your tongue off with it. So don't try it, and don't dare your friends to try it!

If you do have trouble with anything freezing outside in winter, you should pour warm water on it to help melt it.

113: Moss only grows on the north side of trees.

MYTH SCALE: 2

About the myth: Go out for a hike in the woods and find moss growing on a tree. Chances are it's on the north side of the tree. The proof is right there!

The truth: Yes, moss does often grow on the north side of trees, but it can grow wherever it's shady. So look a little harder to see if you can find it growing on other sides as well. The reason it likes growing on the north side the most is because of the way Earth is tilted toward the sun. In the Northern Hemisphere the north gets less sun than the south. But if you were to go to the Southern Hemisphere, where the south gets less sun, you'd see that moss grows more on the south side of trees!

The takeaway: If it's a shady enough area, moss will grow on any side of a tree. Do your own little experiment: Go for a hike and see where you can find moss growing.

Additional facts: Moss is kind of a weird plant. It's considered a non-vascular plant, and it doesn't have any roots. It needs a lot of water since it doesn't have roots to drink up water like most plants. So in addition to looking for moss in shady spots, look in damp areas too.

Luck Legends

A RABBIT'S FOOT WILL BRING YOU GOOD LUCK.

It's kind of gross when you think about it. Will having a rabbit's foot bring you luck? This legend has been around for hundreds of years. It's supposed to bring you luck and keep away evil things, but don't go looking for a rabbit to try this for yourself. You can sometimes find these good-luck charms for sale, but don't worry if you're concerned about the rabbit. Chances are it's not real.

114: Gardening only happens in spring and summer.
MYTH SCALE: 3

About the myth: From the "Autumn" section, we know that you can grow and plant things in the autumn. But what about winter? No one gardens in winter, right?

The truth: Let's start with outdoor gardening. Lots of plants are still growing outside in winter, and it's especially a good time of year to have trees and shrubs with berries because the birds love stopping by for a bite to eat. Then look at indoor gardening. You can grow herbs and other plants indoors as long as you have a good sunny window. Lots of people will start their seeds in late winter too, as a way to get a jump-start on spring. Another option is to get started on houseplants in winter. Your garden center will probably have a whole area with house-plants, so go take your pick!

The takeaway: You really can garden year-round. If you're new to winter gardening, go to a garden center in winter and ask them what you can do. Based on where you live, they can give you some good recommendations for your area.

Additional facts: Here's another fun winter garden activity to try: Take an avocado pit or the top of a pineapple and put it in a jar. See if you can get it to root. Chances are you're not going to grow a whole new plant, but it's a fun experiment to try.

YOU CAN TELL HOW OLD A TREE WAS BY COUNTING THE RINGS OF A STUMP.

There is a whole branch of science dedicated to studying tree rings. It is called dendrochronology, and there is way more to it than counting tree rings. Trees add rings each year as they grow bigger and bigger. The outer layer of the tree is called the bark, and this protects the tree. The phloem (FLOH-em) and xylem (ZI-lem) let nutrients and water move through the tree. Between these layers is the cambium layer, the part of the tree that grows. This means the oldest tree rings are at the center of the tree trunk. Dendrochronologists (tree ring scientists) examine the rings of numerous different trees in an area to understand the past. Wide rings can indicate good growing conditions, while narrow rings result from drought or other stressors. Sometimes fires burn the bark, but they don't kill the tree. These fire scars can help researchers understand how often fires burned historically.

Researchers can core out a sample section of tree so they can count the rings without cutting the tree down.

115: Having indoor plants will make you healthier.

MYTH SCALE: 2

About the myth: Plants are great because they help purify the air around them. In turn, just a single houseplant can make you a lot healthier because it's giving you better-quality air.

The truth: Indoor plants do help make the air around you healthier, so that part is true. But here's where it gets trickier: Just one plant won't do much good at all. To really make a difference, you need lots and lots of plants in a little space. This is because one plant alone can't really do much in a big room. You can load up on plants if you want, but just remember that more is better.

The takeaway: An indoor plant or two isn't going to automatically make you healthier—that's a pretty bold statement! Plants just make us happier more than anything, which is why lots of people have indoor plants. If you really want to be around plants to be healthier, the best thing you can do is get outside around trees, shrubs, flowers, and other living things. You know how they say fresh air is great? That's true!

Additional facts: You have to be careful about indoor plants sometimes being toxic to animals. Lots of cats like to munch on plants, so if you have animals and want to have houseplants, you might want to do a little research first so you don't make them sick. If you do have a cat, sometimes you can find little catmint plants or grass you can grow indoors specifically for them to munch on. Ask your local garden center—it's fun to try, and your cat will probably love you for it.

116: Owls can spin their heads all the way around.

MYTH SCALE: 2

About the myth: Even if you haven't seen an owl in person, you've probably seen books or movies where the owl is looking straight ahead and then it rotates it's head all the way around. It seems to rotate in a full circle. Now that's like having eyes in the back of your head!

The truth: Owls can rotate their heads a lot—most species can make it about 270 degrees! However, they can't quite rotate their heads all the way around (which would be 360 degrees). There's a good reason owls can rotate their heads so much. The way their eyes work makes it very difficult for them to see things around them. You know how you can keep your head still and move your eyes around to see what's around you? Owls can't really do this, so they rely on moving their heads instead. It works great—owls are known for being good hunters, and a lot of that is because of their great eyesight.

The takeaway: It might look like owls can rotate their heads all around—after all, 270 degrees is pretty impressive. It's not quite *all* the way around though. If you get the chance to see an owl in person—either in the wild or at a zoo or something—take a close look to see how far they rotate.

Additional facts: Want another quirky fact about owls? Many owls have feathers on the top of their heads that look like ears, but they're actually called tufts! Look up a picture of a great horned owl to see an example of this.

117: All birds migrate somewhere else for winter.

MYTH SCALE: 2

About the myth: Everyone knows that birds migrate in autumn. Then by winter you might have some new birds in your backyard that came from the north, but they are definitely different than the birds you had in your area a few months ago.

The truth: Lots of birds do migrate, but there are a whole group of birds that are considered year-round residents. This means you could have the same cardinal or blue jay at your feeder throughout the year. The best way to figure out which birds are year-round and which ones migrate is to get a good field guide birding book. All field guides will include a range map with the bird, which is color-coded. At a glance, you can easily see if a bird is in your area year-round or not. And remember that a bird's range from one area to another can be quite different. A bird in the South can be there year-round while it's only a summer resident in the North.

The takeaway: It all depends on the bird and where you live. The next time you see a bird outside in winter, take the time to look it up in your field guide. You can see if it's year-round in your area or not.

Additional facts: A lot of people think robins migrate south for winter, but they are one of the birds that can stay in one area year-round. You might not think of robins hanging out in the snow, but they can!

CREATE YOUR OWN CLOUDS

It's hard to study clouds when they're so far away, but now you can make your own in a jar. It's a simple way to study the weather. Maybe your teacher would even let you show this experiment to your class at school.

Supplies: Jar, black paper, tape, matches, ice, baggie

Time: 10 minutes

Observe and learn: Watch how the clouds form as the hot and cold air meet. The same thing happens outside. See if you can notice how the clouds in your jar look similar to the clouds in the sky.

How-To:

1. Make sure the jar you use is nice and clean. A gallon-size jar works great. Then tape a strip of black construction paper around the bottom half of the jar. This will make the clouds easier to see.
2. Pour a couple of inches of warm water into the bottom of the jar.
3. Next have an adult take the open jar and hold a lit match over the mouth for a few seconds. They should then drop the match inside.
4. Immediately cover the top of the jar with a baggie filled with ice cubes. You don't want them to fall in, so make sure you have enough ice so that you can gently lay it on top.
5. Watch how fog and clouds start to form little by little. Leave the ice there until the clouds start to go away. Then repeat the experiment. Test out whether clouds form more quickly if you use hotter water.

There are several different types of clouds. The ones you're creating in this experiment are like stratus clouds, while the big puffy ones are called cumulous clouds.

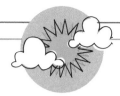

Weather Legends

IF YOU SEE A SQUIRREL QUICKLY GATHERING NUTS, SNOW IS ON THE WAY.

This one makes sense—you would expect an animal to be able to detect bad weather a little bit. So why wouldn't a squirrel try to gather up a bunch of nuts and food before it snows? Here's another legend where the animal isn't necessarily predicting the weather. It's just reacting to signs around it. Test this out for yourself. Watch your bird feeders before it snows and see if you notice more birds and squirrels trying to gather a bit to eat.

118: Plants can't grow without soil.
MYTH SCALE: 1

About the myth: When it comes to plants, it's relatively simple. They need soil, water, and sunshine to survive. Doesn't this pretty much sum things up?

The truth: While most plants do in fact need soil, there are some exceptions to this rule. For example, moss (as mentioned earlier in this section) doesn't have roots. It can grow on rocks and on trees, so it doesn't need soil at all. Then there are a group of plants called air plants that don't need soil either! They grow (often in trees) just in the air!

The takeaway: Most plants do better with soil, so don't think you don't need soil to garden. There are a few exceptions though. Find out which ones are good ones to try, and see if you can grow plants without soil!

Additional facts: In winter you can always find kits for growing amaryllis, paper whites, and other bulbs inside. Some of these kits have little soil starters, but others just have you growing them in rocks or marbles! It sure makes it pretty, growing plants in a clear vase. Then you can see the roots too. Try one of these plant kits this time of year.

119: Wolves howl at the moon.

MYTH SCALE: 3

About the myth: One of the most typical and picturesque night scenes related to animals is that of a wolf and a moon. The wolf usually has its nose pointed up into the sky where there's a full moon, and it's letting out a long, soulful howl.

The truth: This myth has been circulated for years and years. No one is exactly sure where it got started, but there are a lot of ancient stories, pictures, and art related to wolves from all over the world. Wolves are pretty common—you can find them all over the world except Antarctica and South America, so it's no wonder so many cultures have embraced this animal. But the truth of the matter is, they don't really howl at the moon.

The takeaway: Wolves might howl at night, and they might even howl when there's a full moon. But they are not purposefully howling at the moon. It's still fun to hear wolves howling at night though. What do you think they're howling at?

Additional facts: Wolves are actually very similar to dogs, and they communicate in a lot of similar ways. They will howl, bark, whine, whimper, and more. Another important thing to note about wolves is that some populations are expanding while others are on the endangered species list.

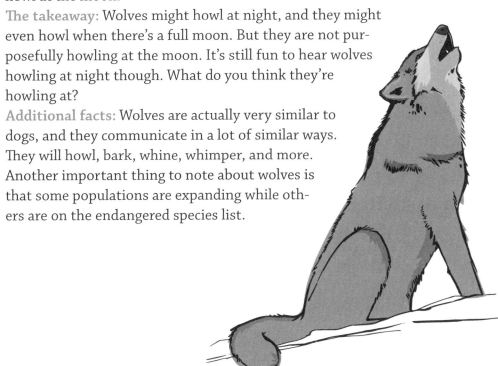

120: Talking or singing to plants helps them grow.
MYTH SCALE: 2

About the myth: If you talk or sing to your plants, they are going to grow better, faster, and stronger. Either way, it can't hurt to try, so you might as well.

The truth: This myth is another tricky one because many people swear by it. The thing is, plants need carbon dioxide, which comes out when you talk, sing, or simply breathe. So people believe that if you talk more to your plant, it will get more carbon dioxide and thrive. They think this is especially good for indoor plants. Now, there have been several studies done on this, and some scientists say it really can make a difference, but there's not enough evidence to say for sure.

The takeaway: Again, it doesn't hurt to talk or sing to your plants. So if you want to, go right ahead. But you shouldn't expect your plants to shoot up in growth because of it. Even if it does help a little, it's not going to make that big of a difference in the grand scheme of things. This is why this one should really stay on the myth list. It's deceiving to think you can make plants grow just by talking to them!

Additional facts: This is a great experiment to try for yourself or in your classroom. Ask your teacher if you can try a plant experiment at school. Have two pots in which you plant seeds. Then have your classmates talk to just one of the pots every day. What's your conclusion?

Be a Scientist

EXPERIMENT WITH MIXING COLORS TOGETHER

If you mix green and yellow together, what color will you get? Even if you know the answer, it's fun to do a little experimenting to find out. Get out your food colors or paint set to put the colors to the test.

Supplies: Food coloring, clear cups, plastic spoons, water, paint
Time: 15 minutes
Observe and learn: After you've mixed together several options, try mixing 3 together to see what it makes. Challenge yourself to make colors like pastel orange, light pink, and turquoise too.

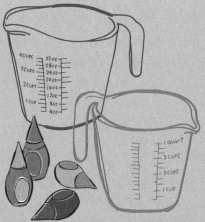

How-To:

1. This is a pretty simple exercise. The preparation will take the most work. Think of it like dyeing Easter eggs, except without the eggs. Use clear plastic cups. Set them up all in a row, filled halfway full of water.
2. One at a time, mix two colors in each cup and mix slowly with the plastic spoon. Make notes as you go with each cup.
3. Try different options. Maybe mix three droplets of yellow with one droplet of green. Then add two more of green. Notice how the shades change as you add more food coloring.
4. Don't forget to try a few different scenarios where you add three or more colors just to see what happens.
5. Once you've experimented with water, get out a simple water-based paint set and try mixing colors this way too. You'll need a cup of water to keep your paintbrush clean. Have fun!

It's hard to make black. If you mix all the colors together, you'll just get a dark brown.

121: There are nine planets in the solar system.

MYTH SCALE: 2

About the myth: For years and years kids at school have been learning about the nine planets in our solar system, starting with those closest to the sun. The order goes like this—Mercury, Venus, Earth, Mars, Jupiter, Saturn, Uranus, Neptune, and Pluto.

The truth: If you ask most people, they will still say we have nine planets, but scientists don't really agree anymore. There's some disagreement as to whether or not Pluto is a "real" planet. Some are calling it a dwarf planet now. Since the Pluto controversy started around 2005, scientists are starting to discover what they think could be other smaller planets in the solar system.

The takeaway: While there's still a lot of discussion happening around this subject, one thing is certain: The days of nine planets are probably long gone. The solar system is a tricky thing to study because it's so far away, but scientists are making a lot of progress. Keep watching and listening for news about space. Who knows how many planets we could end up with?

Additional facts: Even if Pluto got demoted, it's still worth studying. Here are a few fun facts about Pluto. It's actually smaller than Earth's moon. Because it is so far away, Pluto revolves around the sun much slower than Earth does. In fact, while it takes Earth one year to orbit the sun, it takes Pluto around 248 years.

FROGS CAN FREEZE IN THE WINTER.

Winter is a difficult season for many animals. But have you ever thought about how frogs and toads survive winter? They will often experience a hibernation-like state during cold weather where their metabolism slows down. Aquatic species usually spend the winter on the bottom of a pond or stream. Terrestrial species will sometimes bury themselves underground below the frost line. Other places to overwinter include cracks and crags in logs, rocks, or deep in the leaf litter. Frogs and toads in these locations can freeze during the winter. The frogs and toads will have ice crystals inside the body, but high levels of glucose in the frog's organs prevent these from freezing altogether so it keeps them alive.

In the tropics, some amphibians will estivate during the long dry season. This is kind of like hibernation during hot weather.

122: Bald eagles are rare.

MYTH SCALE: 2

About the myth: Back in the 1970s, eagles were almost wiped out! Pesticides were causing eagle eggshells to break before the babies could hatch. This led to population declines, and they were put on the endangered species list. This means it's pretty rare and unique to see a bald eagle, so you should treasure those moments if you spot one.

The truth: You definitely should treasure a bald eagle sighting—that's cool! But these great birds are no longer endangered. Conservation efforts over the past several decades have helped them prosper. Now bald eagles are thriving across the country. Areas that haven't seen bald eagles for years are now having these birds nest and come back year after year. Back in the 1970s, they said there were fewer than 500 nests in the lower forty-eight states. In 2007 they removed the bald eagle from the endangered species list, and now it's estimated that more than 10,000 eagle pairs are nesting.

The takeaway: This is a true success story of people who set out to save the bald eagle. This bird is the national symbol of the United States after all, so it was definitely a worthwhile effort. The next time you spot an eagle, remember that it took a lot of work to get the population strong again. Maybe you can be a part of helping an endangered species make a comeback!

Additional facts: Bald eagles will often nest in the same place, year after year, with the same mate. They keep building and adding to their nest each year, so it can get pretty big. Some eagle nests can weigh 2 tons or more!

123: Deserts are always hot.

MYTH SCALE: 2

About the myth: You've probably seen pictures in books or scenes in movies where someone is trudging through the desert. It's hot and dry, and the heat seems unbearable. Yep, this is the traditional desert. It's always hot.

The truth: The definition of a desert has more to do with rainfall and less to do with heat. Deserts are large areas of land that get very little rainfall throughout the year (less than 16 inches, to be exact). This can include very hot areas, especially in areas of the Southwest and California. However, even these areas can get cool temperatures. Some deserts can get to be over 100 degrees Fahrenheit during the summer days and then drop to freezing at night in the winter. But in general, not all deserts are hot or are in hot climates. For instance, the famous Gobi Desert in Asia gets very cold in winter. Even deserts in the United States are chilly sometimes. Also, areas of Antarctica are technically considered deserts based on the little amount of rainfall they receive, and it's definitely not very hot there!

The takeaway: If you're going to the desert, make sure to check the temperature during the day and at night, because you might need a jacket! Even more importantly, make sure you have plenty of water, because all deserts are dry, and you're definitely going to need to stay hydrated.

Additional facts: Many people associate sand with deserts, but this isn't always the case. In fact, scientists estimate that only 20 percent of deserts in the world are covered with sand.

124: Birds need you to feed them in winter or they can't survive.

MYTH SCALE: 3

About the myth: During warmer months, birds eat a lot of insects. They also eat a lot of plant material. So when it gets cold, they don't really have a lot of food sources to go to. This is why they need you to keep the feeders full so they can survive even during the coldest temperatures.

The truth: Scientists have done a lot of study on birds, and they've actually discovered that birds would be just fine (even in the winter) whether we feed them or not! Of course, there are many other reasons to feed birds. It's cool to have these creatures of the wild come into our own backyards where we can observe them up close. But if you're feeding birds in the winter and you forget to fill the feeders for a little while, don't worry, because they'll be just fine! It is like when your favorite restaurant closes—you'll still be able to find a place to eat.

The takeaway: Birds don't rely on us, but it doesn't hurt to feed them either. If you want to offer a good food source in winter, you could put out suet. And if you're wondering which seed to feed them (there are a lot of different options out there), start out with a basic feeder filled with black-oil sunflower seeds. This is a good-quality seed that will attract many birds.

Additional facts: Don't forget the importance of offering birds water in winter. Water can freeze in winter, so you might have to refill it frequently, or you could get a heater for your birdbath too.

MOUNT WASHINGTON HAS THE WORST WEATHER IN THE UNITED STATES.

Hundreds of thousands of people visit the summit of New Hampshire's Mount Washington each summer, but in winter the mountain is an extreme place to be. Lots of places claim to have the worst weather, but Mount Washington can back up this claim with years of weather data. At 6,288 feet elevation, the mountain peak is the highest in the northeastern United States. With near-constant winds whipping, winter can set in in October and linger well into April. The surrounding geography puts the mountain directly in the path of many storms. The peak gets the brunt of extreme cold, wet, windy, and icy conditions. The low visibility and rugged terrain make it especially treacherous. On average the wind blows at 35 miles per hour year-round, and the annual accumulation of snow, ice pellets, and hail is 281.2 inches. No doubt about it, that is some bad weather.

The highest wind speeds recorded on Mount Washington were 231 miles per hour and occurred in 1934.

125: The sun is yellow.

MYTH SCALE: 2

About the myth: Don't look directly at the sun, but go outside on a sunny day and take a look up in the sky. See what color the sun looks like to you. It's yellow, right? Of course it is! Everyone knows this. It's why kids everywhere reach for the yellow crayon whenever they're drawing a picture of the sun.

The truth: Wait a minute now. Perhaps the sun isn't bright yellow—a lot of people say that it's orange or red. Is this right? Nope, it's not yellow, orange, red, or any combination of those colors. Well, it might look like it to us, but that's just the way it appears as its light passes through Earth's atmosphere. If you were to take a trip to space and look at the sun, you would see that it's actually white!

The takeaway: While the sun isn't actually yellow, it's probably still OK to use that yellow crayon when you're coloring because that's how it looks to humans. Besides that, have you ever checked out a sunset with gorgeous colors of orange, pink, gold, and other colors? Now that's worth capturing on camera.

Additional facts: Everyone knows that the sun is the largest object in the solar system, right? It's technically considered a star (did you know that?), and it takes up the most mass of the whole solar system. Jupiter takes up the second most.

126: You can only see the northern lights in the north.

MYTH SCALE: 2

About the myth: Have you heard about the northern lights? They are one of the coolest occurrences in nature. And since *northern* is in the name, you must need to be in the north in order to see them.

The truth: When the northern lights appear in the sky at night, they light it up with gorgeous colors like turquoise, blue, purple, and more. They seem to sweep across the sky like someone took a paintbrush from top to bottom. Being in the north doesn't guarantee you'll see these lights though. A lot goes into whether you'll be able to see the northern lights, including location and time of year. These are huge factors, but overall, you don't have to be in the north to see them.

The takeaway: Some of the best options for seeing the northern lights include going to places like northern Canada and Alaska, so these are definitely places in the north. But the northern lights can be seen as far south as Pennsylvania and Wisconsin. And in some rare years, they can be seen even farther south than that! (So maybe it depends on your definition of north!) If you have a dream to see the northern lights, do a little research on where you need to go and what time of year to be there.

Additional facts: Northern lights are actually considered a type of aurora. Aurora lights occur around the northern and southern magnetic poles and are caused by solar flares of electrically charged particles entering Earth's atmosphere.

Luck Legends

This is a pretty confusing myth. Some cultures claim peacock feathers are beautiful and are lucky. Others claim they bring bad luck and you shouldn't possess them at all! Either way, take a moment to study a peacock feather sometime. It has an incredible amount of detail and pattern in it. Of course, the colorful feathers most people refer to are from males. The females aren't very colorful birds at all.

127: Animals can only see in black and white.
MYTH SCALE: 2

About the myth: You might have heard that dogs only see in black and white. Then this must be true for other animals too!

The truth: Let's start with dogs—they don't just see black and white. Dogs, like many animals, still see colors, but they just don't see as many colors as humans do. Animal eyes have fewer cones than most humans. For instance, they are missing the red cone, so red and green look the same to them. All animals are different though. For instance, deer don't see orange like we do—this is why hunters in the woods can wear bright orange and the deer don't seem to notice.

The takeaway: It can vary a lot from one animal to another, but the bottom line is that most animals can see colors.

Additional facts: Some animals can even see better than humans because they have more eye cones. For instance, some snakes, butterflies, and birds are believed to have excellent eyesight and might be able to see colors that we can't.

128: You can't wake a hibernating animal.

MYTH SCALE: 2

About the myth: Hibernation is common in animals during winter. It involves animals going into a deep sleep, so for several weeks they can go without food. Even if you tried to wake up an animal, it would just keep right on sleeping.

The truth: Hibernation varies so much from one animal to the next. And for most animals, if you tried hard enough, you could wake them up. Still, it's a pretty amazing thing in general. Hibernation involves an animal usually going into a protected space like a burrow or a den and then lowering its metabolism. Animals don't necessarily sleep away the whole winter like some people think, but they are able to go long periods of time with relatively little food. Other species will go into a daily torpor, which is kind of like an overnight hibernation.

The takeaway: The bottom line is that you shouldn't disturb an animal at all, whether it's hibernating or not! And if you did, the animal would probably wake up. There's so much more to learn about hibernation and how it's different from one animal to the next. Do some more research on your own so you can amaze your friends!

Additional facts: Some species automatically go into a seasonal hibernation, while other species might just slow down their metabolism during harsh conditions.

129: Birds only nest in spring.
MYTH SCALE: 2

About the myth: Spring signifies new life. It's the time of year for birds to start building their nests. You can see them out and about, singing and flitting from one tree to the next as they gather nesting material and prepare to lay eggs and raise babies.

The truth: Spring does mark the start of nesting season for many birds, but the truth is that some birds start earlier, even in winter! Owls are especially known for this. They will start nesting as early as January or February, depending on the area. They start building their nests and laying their eggs even when there's snow on the ground in some cases. Although they don't nest until later in the year, ducks are birds that start choosing mates in winter as well.

The takeaway: Spring isn't the only time for nesting birds. When you're out and about this winter, keep an eye out for owls and ducks to see if you notice them exhibiting signs of nesting. These might include males and females hanging out together more, or the birds gathering nesting material. You can also listen for owls calling to one another.

Additional facts: Most owls and ducks don't use birdhouses, but a couple of them do. Screech-owls and wood ducks both will. Of course, you'll need the right habitat. Owls needed wooded areas, and wood ducks need to be by water. If you don't live in these types of areas, don't be discouraged. Instead, use it as an excuse to go out looking for birds instead.

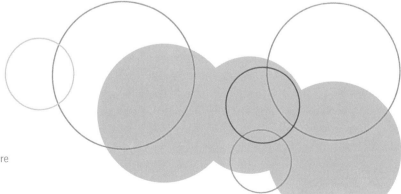

MALE SEAHORSES CARRY THE BABIES.

For most fish, parental care is often lacking. The eggs are fertilized in the water and left to develop and hatch on their own. While seahorses aren't going to get any "parent of the year" awards, they do offer a bit of added protection early on. The males have a specialized pouch where the eggs are deposited. It depends on the species, but there can be anywhere between a few dozen to thousands of eggs. A few hundred is most common. The eggs take at least a week, and in some species up to forty-five days, to develop. Once the baby seahorses hatch, the male squeezes them from his pouch. Don't go handing out "father of the year" awards though. These tiny seahorse babies are immediately left to fend for themselves.

The slowest fish in the world is the dwarf seahorse. It moves at just 0.001 mile per hour.

130: The brain is the largest organ.

MYTH SCALE: 3

About the myth: Think about your body for a moment and the organs inside. The head is pretty large, and the brain fits inside, so it must be the largest organ.

The truth: Are you ready for this? The brain isn't the largest organ. It's not even the second-largest organ! It's the third-largest organ. By the way, the skin is the largest organ and the liver is the second. It's still a very essential part of the human body though. The brain has one hundred billion cells, which help control all the actions of our bodies! Now that's a pretty important and essential job.

The takeaway: The brain might not be the largest organ, but it's certainly one of the most important. We rely on it every single day to keep our bodies moving and functioning.

Additional facts: Want to know another organ that is large and just as important as the brain? Any guesses? It's the heart! It's the fifth-largest organ in the body, and without it, you wouldn't be able to survive at all.

Weather Legends

BIRDS CAN PREDICT AN EARTHQUAKE.

Earthquakes are one of those things that are really unpredictable. They come and go so suddenly. So it's pretty amazing to think that birds might be able to predict them. Of course, there's no real scientific evidence that backs this up. There are some examples that show birds flying away once an earthquake occurs, but not necessarily before. It's not clear where this legend started, but if you do happen to experience a small earthquake, look to see how the animals around you are reacting.

Be a Scientist

TEST OUT HOW MUCH WATER EXPANDS

When water freezes it expands, right? It's fun to see it happen right before your own eyes. With this water balloon experiment, you can make colorful ice balls while being a scientist at the same time.

Supplies: Water, balloons (10 or more), food coloring, tape measure
Time: 15 minutes prep; a day to freeze solid
Observe and learn: Measure how much water expands. Also test out how quickly it freezes. How much faster will something free in 0-degree weather versus 20-degree weather?

How-To:
1. Take a balloon and stretch the opening so it's nice and wide. Add a few droplets of food coloring to each balloon.
2. Now add water to the balloons. Remember, the bigger you make your ball, the longer it will take to freeze.
3. Once you have the water in, swish it around a bit to make sure the food coloring completely dyes the water. Then use a flexible tape measure to see how big the balloons are.
4. Place the balloons in the freezer, or outside if it's cold enough. Let them sit at least overnight so they freeze solid.
5. The next morning measure the balloons again to see how much they expanded. Then cut away the balloons, leaving a colorful icy ball. Now decorate your yard.

Do another test to see how long it takes for the ice balls to completely melt.

131: Swallows survive the winter by burrowing in mud.

MYTH SCALE: 3

About the myth: Before researchers knew so much about bird migration, there were lots of ideas to try to explain where some of the birds disappeared to for winter. One theory was that birds, especially swallows, buried themselves in the mud to survive the winter. Lots of things winter underground. So they thought swallows did too.

The truth: Some species of swallows nest in cliffs and riverbanks. This means they spend part of their lives underground. But they don't hibernate down there. Other swallows build nests of mud. In the springtime they can be seen gathering mud in their bills. It is easy to imagine that the swallows are digging themselves out of the mud, but that isn't the case. Instead of wintering in the mud, swallows migrate to the southern United States and as far south as South America.

The takeaway: Swallows are insect eaters, so they spend the winter in warmer climates where they can find food. They don't hibernate, and they certainly don't burrow underground for winter.

Additional facts: Swallows are not the only birds that nest underground. Kingfishers also nest in burrows. These nests can have added protection from the rain as well as predators.

132: You can't be as active in winter as you are in summer.

MYTH SCALE: 3

About the myth: Summer offers opportunities for so many activities, including swimming, biking, and hiking. Even spring and fall in most areas offer good opportunities to be outside and active. Winter, though, is tricky. It just doesn't offer as many possibilities.

The truth: The season is what you make of it. For many people, there are still lots of possibilities to get outside and be active in winter. For people who like winter sports, they can go cross-country skiing, sledding, snowshoeing, and more. Even if those aren't for you, you can do a lot of the same things in winter as you can in other seasons—you just need to be prepared. This might mean wearing several layers or an extra pair of socks in some cases.

The takeaway: You can be active in winter. Get out there and make the most of the season no matter what. Now you might also have to be a little more creative in what you do outside. If you're used to playing kickball in the backyard, you might have to invent a whole new game of "snow ball" instead. Then again, not everyone gets snow in winter, but it doesn't matter. Find reasons to go outside. You won't regret it.

Additional facts: Here's a quirky winter sport that you might not know about at all. It's called curling. It's even an Olympic sport! It involves big, heavy stones that you push across the ice. See if you have a curling club in your area, and look for an open-house event. Maybe you can try this unique sport out for yourself.

133: You lose most of your body heat through your head.
MYTH SCALE: 2

About the myth: If you're going to go outside on a cold winter day, you better make sure to have a hat on. When you lose most of your body heat through your head, it's absolutely essential!

The truth: So where did this myth get started? It looks like its origins date back to the 1970s when a US Army manual said that you need to wear a hat because you lose 40 to 45 percent of your body heat through your head. This came from a study done on soldiers in the cold where they weren't wearing hats. Of course, the soldiers without hats were colder, but this doesn't mean that's the main source of losing heat! Yes, scientists say your face, head, and chest are more sensitive to the cold, but that doesn't mean you lose additional heat from those areas.

The takeaway: It might feel like you're losing more heat through the top of your head if you don't have a hat on, but that's not the case at all. If you were wearing a hat but had on shorts, it would feel like you were losing heat from your legs. Still, you should wear a hat (and pants) in cold temperatures because every little bit helps. Make sure to cover up as much of your skin as possible so you can stay nice and toasty.

Additional facts: Have you ever tried those little hand or foot warmers that you heat up in the microwave? Yes, they really do work. They help your body temperature stay a little bit warmer overall, so if you tend to get really cold outside, give them a try.

IF YOU TALK ON THE MOON, NOBODY CAN HEAR YOU.

The conditions on the moon are far different than here on Earth. For one thing there is no air in space. Since many sounds, including the human voice, are vibrations of air, this means that if you are saying something on the moon, nobody can hear a word you are saying. When you hear a sound on Earth, what you are actually hearing is movements of particles of air. So how can we hear astronauts? Radio waves and light waves can travel freely in space. Astronauts can communicate with one another and with mission control because they are using radio waves to send the "sounds."

In the summer of 1969, *Apollo 11* was the first mission to send people to the moon.

134: Porcupines can throw their quills.

MYTH SCALE: 3

About the myth: Have you (or your pet) ever gotten stuck by porcupine quills? If so, it seems like the quills just reached out and grabbed you right? Almost like you didn't even touch the animal, but instead that the porcupine threw its quills at you. But can porcupines really toss their quills like little spears?

The truth: Porcupine quills are easily dislodged from the porcupine and into whatever they come into contact with. But the animals can't throw their quills. You should still give a porcupine plenty of space though. Porcupines can have over 30,000 quills, which are really considered modified hairs. They are extra stiff, and they come to a very fine tip. The tips of the quills have hundreds of microscopic barbs on them. This makes them extremely difficult to remove from flesh. If you are lucky enough to see a porcupine, take a couple of pictures, but then let it waddle away or climb up a tree.

The takeaway: You might not even see the porcupine quills under the rest of the long hairs, but if the porcupine feels threatened, it will raise up its quills. You might even hear the quills rattling together. Porcupines can release an odor when threatened too. This is similar to what skunks do. No matter how cornered the porcupine feels, it can't throw the quills at a threat.

Additional facts: Porcupine quills take half as much pressure to puncture skin as needles, so researchers are examining them in an attempt to make better needles and staples for medical use.

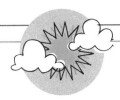

Weather Legends

This legend is especially popular with kids who are hoping for a snow day off from school. Some say you should just put a spoon under your pillow, and that's all it takes. But then others take it a step further and say you should also wear your pajamas inside-out to make it work too. What do you think? Is it worth a try?

135: Ostriches bury their heads in the sand.
MYTH SCALE: 3

About the myth: Everyone knows this one is true. Many people have seen this one with their own two eyes. They look up to see one of these giant birds with its head in the sand.

The truth: This has been circulated for centuries, so it's one of those myths that a lot of people think is true. It's not though! This myth has a lot to do with how ostriches nest. They nest on the ground and will even dig a large hole to lay and keep their eggs. So think about it—if you see an ostrich from a distance, you can imagine how it might look like it has its head in the sand. To add to the myth, an ostrich has a pretty small head compared to the rest of its body, so it would especially be difficult to see whether its head is in or out of the sand.

The takeaway: Ostriches don't bury their heads in the sand at all. Sure, it's easy to see how it might look like that at a distance when they are nesting, but it's just not the case.

Additional facts: While they aren't native to North America, ostriches are pretty interesting birds and are common at zoos and even on farms throughout the country. They are native to Africa and are actually flightless birds. They usually weigh between 100 and 300 pounds. They also lay eggs that weigh 3 to 5 pounds. One more interesting thing is that they aren't really known for being smart birds. They have very small heads and even smaller brains!

136: Mountains always have snow.

MYTH SCALE: 2

About the myth: Mountains are wonderful destinations. People love to visit the mountains all year, but winter is especially fun. Strap on some skis or snowshoes and off you go. You can even find snow on the mountains in the middle of summer. They always have snow on them.

The truth: In some mountains you can find snow all year long. But mountains don't always have to have snow. Some peaks rarely experience snow, but that doesn't make them less worthy of being called mountains. Mountains can form in different ways, but they are areas that are higher in elevation than their surroundings. Sometimes this can mean isolated mountains or it can be an entire mountain range.

The takeaway: This highest mountain peaks will experience snow, but some of the lower mountains don't. The Appalachian Mountains are some of the oldest mountains. They used to be much higher in elevation but have slowly eroded down. The southern parts of the Appalachians extend into Georgia, and these mountains don't have any snow for much of the year.

Additional facts: The highest peak in the United States is Denali in Alaska. Denali has an elevation of 20,236 feet. By comparison, the highest point in Florida is Britton Hill at 345 feet.

BATS ARE THE ONLY MAMMALS THAT CAN FLY.

The wings of birds and bugs help make them champions of flight, but for one group of mammals, flight is still an option. Bats! Bat wings are basically skin that is stretched out over modified hands. The skin is usually covered with thin, fine hairs. Bats have long, skinny finger bones, so you can think of the wing as a webbed hand. The bat thumb runs along the top of the wing, while the other fingers support the wing membrane. The wings are strong and flexible, which helps bats cup air and generate added lift. Bats are excellent fliers. Coupled with their echolocation skills, this makes bats well suited as predators of flying insects.

Did you know that just like birds, some bats migrate? Others will hibernate through winter.

Be a Scientist

PUT TOGETHER YOUR OWN FIELD GUIDE

Field guides have been around for decades. They are picture books highlighting different species. In addition to photos or sketches, they often include tons of information about the plants or animals. Most will include the range, which is where they live, and in what seasons you can find them. Field guides can include species throughout the country or regional species. You may or may not have them in your area . . . until now. It's time to make your own neighborhood field guide.

Supplies: A notebook, glue stick, scissors, access to a printer or copier
Time: 30 minutes
Observe and learn: As you go through field guides at the library, make little notes about interesting facts and tidbits. You'll want to keep these notes in your book too.

How-To:

1. First of all, you have to do your research. This is a perfect activity to do at the library. Go to check out the animal, bird, butterfly, and reptile books. Look for field guides or books about the animals in your state. You can pick as few or as many as you want, but it would be a good start to choose ten birds, ten bugs, ten butterflies, and ten mammals to include in your field guide.
2. Go through and either print pictures from the Internet or make copies of the animals you want in your field guide. Write down everything you think is important to know.
3. Use the books you find as a good guide, but don't follow them exactly. Feel free to add notes about these animals that you know or find. Also make note of whether you've seen them in your backyard.

4. Once you have your field guide made, make a goal to see these animals in the next year. You can turn your guide into a journal of sorts and write down the date you saw each animal.

This would make a great gift too. Do some research for a family or friend and make them a field guide for their area.

137: No two snowflakes are alike.

MYTH SCALE: 1

About the myth: Everyone knows that snowflakes are unique. There are no two snowflakes that are alike, right? They are such complicated shapes and patterns that each one is individual and different.

The truth: There is some truth to this one. No two snowflakes are going to experience the same conditions, so they might each be a little different than the others. But there is a pattern in the way water crystals form and a pattern in snowflakes. As you start to pay attention, you'll see similar snowflake shapes. There are big, fluffy snowflakes and small, compact snow pellets. Besides the classic star-shaped flakes, some snowflakes will be platelike, and other times they're more like columns.

The takeaway: Snowflakes are made up of ice crystals, and ice crystals are just water. The way the two hydrogen and one oxygen atoms come together to form ice crystals happens in a regular pattern. This structure means that all snowflakes are made up of six-sided crystals. These crystals can connect to make more complex and unique shapes. The edges of snowflakes can also break off or melt down. So the bottom line is they're sort of similar but different!

Additional facts: Snowflakes are different than sleet. Sleet is frozen raindrops. Snow crystals form in the clouds as water vapor condenses into ice.

138: There are penguins in North America.

MYTH SCALE: 3

About the myth: Penguins are iconic birds of the cold. They survive in cold and blustery conditions in places like the Arctic and Antarctica.

The truth: Of the nearly 700 species of birds that are found regularly in the United States, penguins aren't one of them. If you've ever seen pictures of penguins hanging out with polar bears, you'll know they are fake. Penguins and polar bears live in different parts of the world. Polar bears are in the north and penguins are in the south. (*Arctic* comes from the Greek word for "bear," and *Antarctic* means "without bears.") No penguins live in Alaska or Canada. Come to think of it, polar bears would probably think penguins would taste pretty good for lunch, so maybe this is a good thing.

The takeaway: You can't find penguins anywhere in North America, except in zoos. There is just one species of penguin that lives north of the equator, the Galapagos penguin. Humboldt penguins live along the western coast of South America. The rest of the species live along the southern coasts of South America, Africa, and Australia as well as along the Antarctic coast.

Additional facts: Penguins can't fly, but they are excellent swimmers. They flap their wings similar to flying birds, and this propels them along underwater. Penguins' main food sources are fish, so being great swimmers is key. A final burst of speed helps launch penguins out of the water and back up onto the ice or land. It's like a reverse dive.

139: Polar bears are left-handed.

MYTH SCALE: 3

About the myth: It doesn't matter which is your dominant hand, but are you right-handed or left-handed? It is way more common for people to be right-handed. Only about 10 percent of the world's population is left-handed. But get this—some people are convinced that polar bears are left-handed.

The truth: It is fun to imagine a polar bear using its left paw to accomplish polar bear tasks. But really, scientists haven't observed this to be the case. If anything, polar bears are probably ambidextrous. They use both their left and right paws pretty equally.

The takeaway: Polar bears pretty much use their left and right paws the same. Most polar bear tasks require both paws anyway. Or sometimes no paws at all are needed.

Additional facts: Another rumor about polar bears is that they will cover up their noses so they can sneak up on their prey. The theory is that the black nose will give them away in the snow, but they can hide this behind a white paw. It's fun to think of polar bears playing peekaboo, but it isn't true. They will still pull a surprise attack though. When seals poke up through the ice to breathe, polar bears can be waiting there to eat them.

ANIMALS CAN LIVE UNDER THE SNOW IN WINTER.

Winter can be cold and snowy. This snow is actually a benefit to many species. Small animals like mice, voles, lemmings, and shrews survive the winter underneath the snow. Without it, they could freeze to death. They'll make elaborate tunnels under the snow (called the subnivean zone) and only occasionally venture to the surface.

How can snow keep something warm? The layer of snow helps keep the temperature from getting too cold. Once the snow gets deep enough, the air temperature doesn't really change the temperature below the snow. Birds like ptarmigan and grouse will take advantage of the insulation that snow provides too. They'll roost in the snow or let a snowfall blanket up over the top of them. The snow also adds protection from certain predators, although some predators can pounce through the snow or can follow the prey species underneath.

While not the same as the subnivean zone, female polar bears will give birth in snow caves, usually to twins. The young polar bears are born nearly helpless, but they grow quickly and are fully active and ready to leave the cave in a few months.

140: Mice eat cheese.

MYTH SCALE: 2

About the myth: Have you ever seen a cartoon with a mouse? Chances are there's a piece of cheese nearby because that's what it likes to nibble on. If you have cheese, better watch out, because a mouse might come along to munch on it.

The truth: It's hard to pinpoint where this myth actually started, but it's been repeated time and time again. In reality, mice will eat just about anything. They'll even gnaw on cardboard and paper if that's all that's available. If they had their choice, though, they would eat seeds, fruit, and other sweet items.

The takeaway: Mice will eat cheese if it's all that's available, but they certainly don't prefer it. Still, you shouldn't set out cheese to catch a mouse. If you really want to try to bring one in, you should offer peanut butter instead!

Additional facts: Mice tend to get a bad reputation, and lots of people are afraid of them. They are pretty harmless though. There are more than thirty species of mice, and they range in both size and color. One more fun fact about mice: Their tails are usually as long or even longer than their bodies!

141: Rabbits are rodents.

MYTH SCALE: 3

About the myth: Rodents are small mammals like mice, chipmunks, and squirrels. Some mammals that are small are clearly not rodents. What about rabbits? Aren't they just squirrels with big ears and cotton-ball-like tails?

The truth: About 40 percent of mammal species are rodents, from the pygmy jerboa to the capybara. Rodents thrive around the world, but rabbits aren't in this category! Along with hares, rabbits are lagomorphs. They are different than rodents in a few key ways, especially with regard to their top front teeth. Similar to rodents, lagomorphs have a pair of top incisors. But they also have a second pair of front teeth directly behind these.

The takeaway: Even though rabbits look a lot like many of the rodents, they aren't closely related at all. Rabbits are different than hares in a few key ways as well. Hare babies are born with their eyes open and with hair. They basically hit the ground running. Baby rabbits are furless and have closed eyes. They develop more in a nest before they are able to move about. Some hares, including the snowshoe hare, turn white in the winter and brown in the summer.

Additional facts: Pikas are also lagomorphs. These small mammals look like rabbits with smaller ears. They live in talus slopes or boulder fields in the mountains or the far north. They will gather and store vegetation to eat all winter long.

142: One human year is equal to seven dog years.
MYTH SCALE: 3

About the myth: Have you ever heard that dogs age differently than humans? So when a dog is having its first birthday according to the calendar, it's really turning about 7 years old in "dog years."

The truth: This is not true at all. It's another one of those tricky ones where no one is quite sure how it got started exactly, but it was printed in a textbook in the 1960s, so maybe that's how this rumor really started to spread. It's common to want to relate animals to people and figure out how old they are as compared to humans, but it's just not a matter of "one size fits all." Some dogs can live to be almost 20 years old while other dogs might only live to be about 6 or 7. So if you're trying to figure out how old a dog is compared to a human based on how long they live, it will vary a great deal.

The takeaway: Yes, a puppy matures at a faster rate than a baby. For example, after just a few weeks, a puppy eats on its own and is starting to be pretty independent, whereas a human baby can take years for this to happen. But you can't really assign a specific equation to figure out the age of a dog by comparison. It might sound like a bit of a copout of an answer, but it's really true—it varies!

Additional facts: Dogs are pretty wise. While some species are better known for their smarts than others, experts say they can often understand hundreds of words or phrases.

143: Poinsettias are flowers.

MYTH SCALE: 3

About the myth: Around the holidays you'll probably see lots of poinsettia plants popping up all over the place. In fact, many people refer to them as Christmas flowers. These gorgeous plants really put you in the holiday spirit, and they make great gifts. Who wouldn't want to get these beautiful flowers?

The truth: You might think poinsettias have these big showy flowers, but they really don't. Those big, colorful "petals" that most people think are flowers are actually called bracts. Yep, the poinsettia plant sure does have a lot of people fooled. However, there are actually flowers on the plant. You just can hardly see them because they are really small and hidden beneath the more colorful and popular bracts.

The takeaway: Poinsettias may not live up to their nickname of "Christmas flower," but they are still gorgeous and really brighten up the holidays. You can find these beautiful plants in a huge array of colors, including red, pink, white, and even some that have several colors.

Additional facts: Poinsettias also have the reputation of being poisonous. Actually, they really aren't that poisonous, though they can mildly irritate dogs or cats that might eat the bracts. Still, anytime you have an indoor plant, you should make sure it's pet friendly.

Stranger than Fiction

NIGHT CAN LAST FOR DAYS IN WINTER.

All days have 24 hours in them, but winter has the shortest days and the longest nights. Sunrise and sunset are determined by the earth's tilt and the latitude. The farther north (or south) you are away from the equator, the more extreme the variation. During the winter solstice the amount of daylight is shortest in the north. In fact, in extreme northern Alaska, the sun can be down for nearly two months. In Anchorage, though, there is still over 5 hours of daylight on the shortest day of the year. On the longest day of the year, Anchorage has nearly 20 hours of daylight.

The vernal equinox marks the beginning of spring, and the autumnal equinox kicks off fall.

144: Playing in the cold makes you sick.

MYTH SCALE: 3

About the myth: Mothers and grandmothers are pretty wise. So when they tell you to bundle up when you go outside in the winter so you don't get sick, it's probably best to listen to them. After all, don't moms know best?

The truth: No matter what Mom or Grandma says, you can't get a cold just by being outside or not wearing a hat. The thing is, when you get sick during cold-and-flu season, it is because of a virus. It actually has nothing at all to do with the weather. If it seems like more people get sick in the winter, it's probably true, but it doesn't have to do with weather. It's because people tend to spend more time indoors, and therefore they are in closer proximity for spreading germs.

The takeaway: You should still listen to your mom and your grandma— go ahead and bundle up when you go outside. But this won't keep you from getting sick. Instead, if you're trying to avoid catching a cold this winter, make sure you wash your hands often. This is how to keep those germs away!

Additional facts: Here's another myth related to moms and having a cold: You know how they say you should have chicken noodle soup if you do get sick? No, it doesn't have any super healing powers, but it sure does seem to make you feel better.

Luck Legends

LADYBUGS WILL BRING YOU GOOD FORTUNE.

People seem to love ladybugs. They are pretty cute, friendly bugs, and many legends say they can bring you good luck. This is one of those myths where it can't hurt to try. Go out and explore your backyard to see if you can come across a ladybug. Even if you don't get good fortune from it, you could grab a magnifying glass to get a really close look at one.

INDEX

ABOUT THE AUTHORS

Photo by Jonathan Good/jgoodmedia.com

Stacy Tornio grew up in Oklahoma and has lived in Wisconsin for the last ten years. As editor of *Birds & Blooms* magazine, she is able to share her love of backyard nature with others. Stacy loves gardening (especially growing veggies) and is a master gardener in Milwaukee, where she teaches youth gardening classes in the community. Along with her husband, Steve, Stacy enjoys watching her two children explore nature in their backyard and beyond. One of Stacy's favorite nature memories from childhood is having her own veggie stand at the local farmers' market with her brother.

Ken Keffer was born and raised in Wyoming. A vagabond naturalist, he's done a little bit of everything, from monitoring mice and vole populations and picking up carnivore scat in Grand Teton National Park to researching flying squirrels in the Tongass National Forest of southeast Alaska and monitoring Bactrian camels in Mongolia's Great Gobi Strictly Protected Area. He's also worked as an environmental educator in Wyoming, northern New Mexico, coastal Maryland, along the shores of Lake Erie in Ohio, and in Wisconsin. Ken enjoys birding, floating on lazy rivers, and fly fishing in the mountains out west. One of Ken's favorite nature memories from childhood is building a fort at his grandparents' creek, which he lovingly referred to as Fort Fishy.

Stacy and Ken are also authors of the award-winning FalconGuides book *The Kids' Outdoor Adventure Book: 448 Great Things to Do in Nature Before You Grow Up*. They also encourage kids and families to get outside on a regular basis with their website, destinationnature.net.

DESTINATION NATURE
Adventures from backyard to mountaintop!

The Kids' Outdoor Adventure Book

448 GREAT THINGS TO DO IN NATURE BEFORE YOU GROW UP

NATIONAL OUTDOOR BOOK AWARD WINNER!

DESTINATION NATURE IS...

A WEBSITE FROM AUTHORS STACY TORNIO AND KEN KEFFER DEDICATED TO GETTING MORE KIDS AND FAMILIES OUTSIDE

NEWSLETTER

Enter your email...

SUBSCRIBE

FEATURED POSTS

BLOG, FOODS / APRIL 10, 2014
12 TWISTED S'MORES

S'MORES! Graham cracker, chocolate, and roasted marshmallow...a classic for sure. We've taken this traditional favorite and provided it with a new twist. Actually...

BLOG, GARDENING / JANUARY 28, 2014
FINGERPRINT FLOWER POTS

My sister-in-law made these awesome fingerprint and thumbprint flowers pots for me one year. She snuck my kids over to her house for a...

🌿 THE AUTHORS